500

red wines

500

red wines

the only red wine compendium you'll ever need

Christine Austin

A Quintet Book

Published by Sellers Publishing, Inc.
161 John Roberts Road, South Portland, Maine 04106
For ordering information:
(800) 625-3386 Toll Free
(207) 772-6814 Fax
Visit our Web site: www.sellerspublishing.com
E-mail: rsp@rsvp.com

ISBN: 978-1-4162-0770-2
Library of Congress Control Number: 2009923849
QTT.RIWN

This book was conceived, designed, and produced by
Quintet Publishing Limited
6 Blundell Street
London N7 9BH
United Kingdom

Project Editor: Martha Burley
Designer: Dean Martin
Art Director: Michael Charles
Managing Editor: Donna Gregory
Publisher: James Tavendale

10 9 8 7 6 5 4 3 2 1

Printed in China by SNP Leefung Printers Ltd.

contents

introduction

Grapevines have grown wild for thousands of years. Grape seeds dating back 8,000 years have been found in the area now known as Georgia in Central Europe, while winemaking has certainly been practiced for 5,000 years. Tombs of the pharaohs of Ancient Egypt were decorated with scenes of vines and winemaking, and the Romans even had a textbook to teach viticulture to their newly conquered populations.

Wine is much more than just a drink. Through the centuries it has been traded across borders, and it has been present at treaties between nations and the coronations of kings. The fame of a region can rest on the quality of its wines. Making ordinary wine is easy, but making great wine is a constant challenge, balancing the effects of soil, sunshine, rain, and frost, along with the grape variety, its method of cultivation, and the skill of the winemaker.

Wine reflects the place where its grapes are grown. It captures aspects of the soil and the weather in its flavor. This is known as the terroir. This explains why two wines, made from the same grape variety in different parts of the world, taste different. Wine also captures the essence of the grapes, their rich fruity flavors, the acidity, and the structure, which evolve over time.

When you begin to look at the history of wine, it becomes more than just a drink

There are a wide range of wines covered in this book—varying in flavor, price, and origin

wine selection

With thousands of wine producers in dozens of countries making wines to stack on the shelves of stores and supermarkets, selecting the right wine to go with a simple supper, a grand dinner, or a special occasion can be daunting. This book aims to steer you toward the best wines from around the world, by describing the wine-growing regions, the grapes, and the climate of each, and then selecting some of the best winemakers, their vineyards, and wines, in each area. It is a book that demands no previous knowledge of wine while it takes you on a journey of discovery.

The wines selected are not necessarily the most expensive, but they all have one thing in common—flavor for money. The combination of good grapes and the skill of the winemaker to create fine-tasting wine at whatever price point the occasion demands has been the ultimate criterion for inclusion in this book. While most producers have just one wine listed, the fact that they are included in the book means that they have the ability to make exceptional wines. If you want to explore the world of wine beyond the 500 wines listed, the winemakers featured here are a good place to start.

Prices are indicated by bottle signs, (see price code box, right), which are an approximation only. International currency variations, taxes, and shipping costs may make a wine slightly cheaper or slightly more expensive in your area, but the general rule is that the more expensive wines have more bottle symbols.

Price code

▯ – wines up to $20

▯▯ – wines up to $30

▯▯▯ – wines up to $40

▯▯▯▯ – wines up to $50

▯▯▯▯▯ – wines over $50

how to use this book

Numbered circles on the map refer to the locations of the vineyards

This opening paragraph offers an overall description of the area, including the terrain of the region and the most popular grape variety. It can also give a brief history of wine production in the region

Each wine comes with quick food pairing ideas for the perfect culinary experience

Aconcagua Valley

The Aconcagua Valley is a warm, dry region, where temperatures are somewhat moderated by the twin effects of cool air from the Andes in the east and Pacific breezes in the west. This is very much a red wine region with Cabernet Sauvignon and Syrah doing well. Farther south, and within easy reach of the Pacific, the subregion of Casablanca Valley draws morning fog into the valley. Discovered suitable for vines in the 1980s, new plantings of Pinot Noir show great finesse and elegance. The new and exciting subregion of San Antonio is even closer to the coast yet its rolling hills provide good growing conditions.

Erecting wooden stakes in vineyard, Aconcagua Valley, Chile

Featured wines, with images of the bottles, are chosen because of their archetypal significance in the region—whether of outstanding quality or great value

A vintage wine is one made from grapes that were all or primarily grown and harvested in a single specified year. For these entries, recommended vintage years are listed. Some wines are non-vintage—usually a blend from the produce of two or more years. This is a common practice for sherry or other specialist red wines

25 wines throughout the book have a barrel symbol—this indicates particularly good aging potential

Small bottle icons, out of 5, symbolize the price range of the bottle. See page 9 for key

1 Casa Marin Miramar Vineyard, Syrah, San Antonio

Just 3 miles from the coast and with a sometimes foggy seaview, the blustery vineyards of this small boutique winery are on calcareous clay soil, which produces a blueberry-soaked, peppery-spiced, tight-structured Syrah. This is one of Chile's most exciting new wineries.

Food pairings: Grilled chicken or coq au vin
Vintage years: 2005, 2004, 2003

2 Matetic, Syrah EQ, San Antonio

A small, family-run company producing very impressive wines using biodynamic methods. This is one of Chile's best Syrahs, with intense blackberry fruit laced with spice; a dense, earthy palate; and a long, chocolate-tinged finish.

Food pairings: Charcoal-grilled red meat
Vintage years: 2006, 2005, 2003

3 Amayna, Pinot Noir, San Antonio

Low yields, a cool climate, and a new gravity-fed winery are key factors in this fresh-tasting Pinot Noir. With wild raspberry aromas, dark cherry fruit on the palate, and subtle oak on the finish, it is bigger in flavor than most Chilean Pinots.

Food pairings: Broiled salmon with lentils
Vintage years: 2006, 2005, 2004

4 Viña Leyda Cahuil, Pinot Noir, San Antonio

Just 10 miles from the Pacific, Leyda Valley is buffeted by a cool summer breeze that keeps temperatures down and blows pests away. The result is this crunchy, juicy, strawberry-stashed Pinot Noir, which still has enough depth and complexity to accompany broiled lamb.

Food pairings: Broiled lamb
Vintage years: 2007, 2006, 2005

5 Seña, Aconcagua Valley

A rocky, densely planted, biodynamically run vineyard in the western part of the Aconcagua Valley, where afternoon breezes keep temperatures down. Still young, this iconic wine is dense with layers of black-berried fruit, coffee, spice, and tobacco.

Food pairings: Roast wild duck, or seared beef fillet
Vintage years: 2005, 2003, 2001

1 ||| 2 || 3 ||| 4 || 5 |||||

South America 105

Rows of vines in New Zealand

growing grapes & making wine

Vines

There are many species of vines but the one that is important for wine is *Vitis vinifera*, which means "wine-producing vine." Within this species, there are thousands of individual varieties, and because it naturally mutates over the years, others are being created constantly. Clever scientists also help make new hybrids and crossings to suit particular growing conditions. On the other hand, a great number of varieties are lost each year as regions try to follow fashion and pull up their native, local vines to replace them with well-known, international varieties.

Before the middle of the ninteenth century all vines were planted on their own roots, but around the end of the nineteenth century an aphid pest called phylloxera invaded the vineyards of Europe from the East Coast of America and quickly spread, first through France, Spain, and the rest of Europe and then, with a few notable exceptions, around the world. The pest killed the vines, which had a devastating effect on viticulture around the world.

Eventually a solution was found. *Vitis vinifera* vines were grafted onto the native vines of North America, which were a different species—*Vitis riparia*, *Vitis labrusca*, and others. These grafted vines retained their vinifera characteristics but their roots are able to withstand phylloxera. Some vineyard areas such as South Australia, Chile, and a few vineyards within Europe have resisted phylloxera and so still grow vines on their own roots.

Growing the grapes

Location is a very important factor. To thrive and produce grapes for wine, vines need warmth, sunshine, and water in balance. The main grape-growing regions lie in two bands around the world, between 32° and 51° N and between 28° and 44° S, where temperatures are high enough to ripen the grapes, yet not too hot to retain acidity. Higher altitude vineyards are cooler, particularly at night, which extends the ripening period and allows for more flavor development, so producers in warm wine regions often plant vineyards on hillsides.

Climate affects the way a vine grows. Average temperatures, day-to-night variation, rain pattern, and sunshine hours all affect the way the grapes develop. Grape varieties are selected to suit the climate and microclimate within a region. A warm sunny slope or a chilly hilltop may require different vines and give totally different results.

Soils vary significantly. There are some vineyards that are as stony as beaches and others as rich and lush as a market garden, but essentially vines prefer well-drained, low-fertile soils so their roots can dig deep. Some varieties do better on specific soil types. Merlot likes the drainage and warmth of limestone while Cabernet Sauvignon does better with more clay in the soil. Grape growers work hard to match the right grape variety to the soil they have.

Age is another variable as vines can live for more than 100 years, but their most productive years are between 5 and 25 years. After that the yield steadily declines, but in many cases the quality increases. Grape growers have to balance quality and quantity in their vineyard. "Old vine" wines, usually from vines older than 35 years, signify concentration of flavor.

Pruning and yield must be carefully monitored. If allowed to run wild, vines will produce lots of foliage and little fruit. They must be pruned and trained to produce a viable crop, but in general the more grapes they produce, the lower the quality. Once again, the grape grower has to balance quantity and quality. Many growers cut off and throw away part of the crop before it is ripe to help raise the quality of the remaining bunches. This is known as a "green harvest."

Most vineyards around the world have adopted "sustainable viticulture" standards, which means they use minimal sprays on the vines to treat pests and diseases. One step further is organic, which does not permit any chemical sprays or fertilizers to be used on the vines. Only certain natural products are allowed.

Biodynamic viticulture takes a more holistic view of viticulture and takes account of the movement of the moon, the energy of the earth, and the need for certain composts to help the vines grow stronger.

From grapes to wine

The principle of winemaking is simple—grapes contain a sweet juice, which is fermented by yeast into alcohol. What makes winemaking a skilled job are all the factors that have a fundamental effect on the quality of the wine.

Sorting involves picking out unripe grapes, leaves, and stems.

Crushing properly allows the juice to run out from the grapes, but not so much that the seeds are broken.

Cold soak, also known as pre-fermentation maceration, refers to when grape must is held before fermentation to allow some fruity flavor compounds to develop.

Yeast can be natural or commercial. Natural yeast may give more complexity in the wine. Commercial yeast is very reliable.

Fermentation temperature can have a huge effect on the flavors that develop during fermentation. Most fermentations start cool and heat up over a few days. Cooling coils within the tank control the speed of fermentation.

Malolactic fermentation is a secondary bacterial fermentation that transforms harsh malic acid to lactic acid. Almost all red wines go through this fermentation, often in cask.

Grapes are crushed gently to allow the juice to run out

Aging takes place in wooden casks. Oak, which has a natural affinity with wine, allows a slow interchange of oxygen between the air and the wine, stabilizing tannins and color and adding its own flavor. French, American, and Eastern European oak is used, and each has a different effect. Casks come in a variety of sizes; the usual barrique is 225 liters (around 60 gallons), but larger casks have a more gentle effect on the wine.

Oak chips and staves are a good alternative to expensive oak barrels. They do not have the same oxygen transfer effect, but they do add texture and flavor to a wine. They have been permitted in many winemaking countries for years but only recently have been allowed in Europe for lower grade wines.

Clones
Throughout the book there is mention of clones and clonal selection. This sounds quite sinister but it is not. Imagine two identical twins who look the same, and in most cases act the same, but one could be better at art and the other better at sport. Clonal selection in vines takes those two identical vines and finds out what each is better at—cherry fruit, smaller grapes, better fruit set—and whether one suits a particular site particularly well. In the end the vineyard is stocked with vines that are most suited to that place. The other clones may well do better in another vineyard, or indeed a winemaker may actually encourage clonal diversity —just to build in complexity into the wine.

The aging process in Opus One Winery, California—using American oak barriques

leading grape varieties

Cabernet Sauvignon

Full-bodied, deep-colored, and rich with black currant fruit, Cabernet Sauvignon has been the mainstay of Bordeaux wines for centuries. In the Médoc it achieves glorious complexity, adding notes of cedar box, pencil shavings, tobacco, and black cherry to its range of flavors. It is a hardy, adaptable vine, which is why it has spread around the world, bolstering other grapes and carving out a reputation from Coonawarra to California.

Cabernet Sauvignon adds tannin and structure to a wine, giving it the ability to age and develop. In the vineyard it needs a certain amount of heat and sunshine to ripen it, so it tends to be grown in warmer soils such as the gravel of the Médoc and the sunshine of Chile's Central Valley. Too much heat, however, turns it soft and soupy. Cabernet Sauvignon is often blended with other varieties such as Merlot, Cabernet Franc, and Shiraz.

Grenache

Known as Garnacha in Spain and Grenache in France, this is one of the world's most widely planted red grapes. It needs hot, dry conditions and produces grapes packed with lush, vibrant strawberry and raspberry fruit, with herbal notes overlaid on the fruit. It blends well with Syrah and is the basis of *vins doux naturels* in Banyuls and Maury.

Merlot

This is the "other" red grape variety in Bordeaux. Preferred over Cabernet Sauvignon on the Right Bank of the Gironde in St Emilion, Merlot provides soft, velvety, plush flavors with lower acidity and less tannin than Cabernet. It likes a well-drained but not totally dry soil. It prefers limestone and clay over gravel and it needs careful control if it is not to overproduce. However, Merlot is capable of producing some of the world's most expensive wines. Pomerol's Château Petrus and Château le Pin arc both Merlot-dominated wines—deep, concentrated, and long-lived. Merlot also travels well. It can be pale and interesting in northern Italy, soft and velvety in the south of France, and deep and luscious in California's Napa Valley. Its flavors range from strawberry, raspberry, black currants, and damson plums, often with a note of spice or fruitcake and occasionally mint. Merlot is a good blender—with Cabernet Sauvignon and with other Bordeaux varietals such as Cabernet Franc and Petit Verdot.

Pinot Noir

If there is one grape variety in the world that winemakers strive to master, it is Pinot Noir (image right). At its best it is sensual, ethereal, full of fruit, yet complex in structure. Keywords to describe it range from strawberries, black cherries, violets, and chocolate, in many cases bound together with savory, gamey, forest-floor notes. It reflects the terroir where it is grown more than many other grapes, gathering violets in Vosne-Romanée and cherries in Nuits St Georges. Finding it at its best is a quest that can take years. Pinot Noir is a fickle grape demanding exactly the right conditions for growing and for winemaking to produce its best. It needs well-drained, low-fertility soils and tends to produce more vibrant wines on limestone-based soils. As a vine it travels moderately well, particularly to New Zealand and Oregon, where it produces exceptional wines, and in Chile where the style is more straightforward and fruity. In general, Pinot Noir as a red wine is not blended with other varieties; its flavors are too delicate to blend with others. When Pinot Noir is used in Champagne, it is blended with Chardonnay and Pinot Meunier.

Syrah/Shiraz

This grape is always known as Syrah in France and is usually called Shiraz in Australia, but in the rest of the world the name used often indicates the style of wine that is being made. Syrah is adopted by those who want to make a more floral, peppery, minerally style, while Shiraz indicates a lusher, sweeter, chocolaty wine. Syrah is at home in the Rhône, on the steep slopes of the Côte Rôtie and the hill of Hermitage. It does well in the southern Rhône, often blended with Grenache and other varieties. In Australia it thrives in the heat of the Barossa Valley, producing dark, intense wines, and changes style slightly in McLaren Vale and the Hunter Valley. California has its devoted followers (the Rhône Rangers), while Chile and South Africa are producing quality wines. Winemakers are experimenting with a co-fermentation technique with the white grape Viognier, which increases the aromas and fixes the color of the wine.

Major grape variety	Regions of significance
Cabernet Sauvignon	Bordeaux (Médoc), Coonawarra, California, Chile (Central Valley)
Grenache	Southern Rhône, Roussillon (Banyuls and Maury), Navarra, Priorat
Merlot	Bordeaux (St Emilion and Pomerol), Northern Italy, California (Napa Valley)
Pinot Noir	Burgundy (Nuits St George), New Zealand, Oregon, Chile
Syrah/Shiraz	Rhône, Australia (Barossa Valley, McLaren Vale, Hunter Valley), Chile, South Africa, New Zealand

Pinot Noir grapes in wicker baskets, Burgundy

other major red varieties

Barbera is popular in northwest Italy and in Argentina, and has bright cherry fruit with a twist of acidity. Grown in warm climates it has dense plummy flavors and a touch of spice. Tannins are light- to medium-weight.

Cabernet Franc is related to Cabernet Sauvignon, but it ripens a little more easily, giving lighter, raspberry flavors with touches of red currants and herbs. Used in Bordeaux blends and grown in the Loire as well as in Australia, New Zealand, and California.

Carignan is also known as Carignane (USA), Carignano (Italy), Mazuelo (Rioja), and Cariñena (Spain). This rustic, tannic grape variety needs a warm climate to ripen properly. Usually part of a blend, it adds color and red berry flavors.

Cinsault is widely grown in the south of France. This variety is aromatic and spicy with soft supple fruit. Often used in a blend with Carignan, it needs to be cut back and its yields limited to really give good flavors. Also grown in Lebanon and South Africa.

Gamay (image above left) is the grape variety of Beaujolais. It is light, fresh-tasting, and full of easy-drinking strawberry fruit. It grows best on the granite hillsides of Beaujolais and is often made into wine using a process known as carbonic maceration, which enhances its fruity qualities. Rarely blended, Gamay is also grown in the Loire and in Switzerland.

Malbec is best known for its dark-colored, deep, plummy wines from Argentina. Malbec actually originates in the Cahors region of France. Now that Argentina has

Vineyard in Bacedasco, Piacenza, Emilia-Romagna, Italy, where Barbera is the main regional variety

made it its signature variety, it is recognized for its lush flavors and ripe, structured tannins. Often sold as a single varietal, Malbec is also a useful component in Cabernet Sauvignon and Shiraz blends.

Mourvèdre is deep in color with the taste of wild blackberries and herbs with touches of licorice. Mourvèdre is a grape that needs sunshine and warmth to ripen properly. At home in the south of France, it also grows in Spain, where it is called Monastrell, and in Australia (Mataro). Good in blends with Grenache.

Nebbiolo (image above right) is the grape variety of Barolo and Barbaresco. Nebbiolo is an intense grape, with the scent of roses and the flavor of cherries, mulberries, and spice. Tannic and acidic when young, it needs time to soften and show its truffle and licorice complexity.

Petit Verdot (image above left) forms only a small part of a Bordeaux blend, but this grape is valued for its color, structure, and floral scent. It ripens late and needs a warm year to really show its best. Many growers around the world are experimenting with this grape, in particular in Chile, Australia, South Africa, Spain, and Italy.

Pinotage is a cross between Pinot Noir and Cinsault, created in South Africa in the early twentieth century. It has ripe mulberry and blackberry fruit, overlaid with spice and just a hint of tar. Planted extensively in South Africa, it is also being trialed in other countries such as New Zealand and California.

Sangiovese is the traditional grape variety of Tuscany, grown throughout Italy and characterized by its floral aroma and the taste of ripe Morello cherries with a dusting of herbs. Grown well, with low yields it ages superbly. With high yields it can be thin and acidic.

Tannat is falling in popularity in the Basque region of France, where it contributes color, alcohol, and high levels of tannin to wines such as Madiran. It has found a new home in Uruguay where it ripens well to give juicy, dark, blackberry-flavored wines with fine, structuring tannins. Also starting to appear in Chile and Argentina.

Tempranillo is at the heart of almost all great Spanish wines. Crunchy with raspberry-laden, herb-dusted flavors, it has a lush, succulent texture and ages well. Rioja and Ribera del Duero are its spiritual home, but it crops up under other names such as Tinto Fino, Tinto de Toro, and Cencibel. Also grown extensively in Argentina, South Africa, Australia, and California.

Zinfandel (image above right) is closely related, although not identical to Southern Italy's Primitivo. It has made its home in California, where it produces a range of wines from soft rosés to deep, juicy, spice-laden blockbusters. It likes mineral-rich slopes and needs a long growing season. Also grown in Mexico, Chile, and South Africa.

regional specialties

Chile

Chile's regional speciality is the Carmenère. This grape variety was mislabeled over a hundred years ago. Cuttings were taken in the 19th century from France to Chile and on the voyage the labels were lost, so they called it Merlot. A few years later, the remaining vines in France were virtually wiped out by phylloxera, so the Chilean cuttings were almost the sole survivors. Now correctly labeled, Carmenère has sweet, blackberry, plum, spice, savory, and chocolate flavors. It is good as a single varietal but also adds interest to Cabernet and Merlot blends.

Portugal

One of the great joys of Portugal is that this country has held onto its local varieties. In some cases the vineyards are mixed and are only just now being identified. Key varieties include Touriga Franca which makes scented, fruity wines: Touriga Nacional, recognized as one of Portugal's finest grapes, deep-colored, tannic, and powerful; Tinta Roriz, also known as Aragonez, and the same as Spain's Tempranillo, known for its red fruit flavors and firm tannins; Trincadeira with its bright raspberry fruit; and Alicante Bouchet, a red-fleshed variety that adds color to Alentejo wines.

Greece

Greece has also held onto its native grape varieties. Agiorgitiko, also known as Mavroudi Nemeas or St George, adds color and flavors such as black currants, prunes, and spice to a blend; Xinomavro is grown in the cooler north of Greece and provides acidity and color; Mavrodaphne is most famous for its use in sweet red wines but is increasingly used in dry wines; Krassato is a blending grape grown in northern Thessaly and western Macedonia.

Eastern Europe

While many international grapes are grown in Eastern Europe, many local varieties remain, adding their own character to the wines. Feteasca Neagra is Romania's most famous local red grape variety, producing fruity, juicy wines for early consumption. Kékfrankos is the Hungarian name for the Austrian Blauerfrankish. It produces a deep-colored, sweet, earthy style of wine. Kadarka is Hungary's most widely planted red variety, producing deep-flavored, tannic wines.

Wine-growing near Patras, Peloponnes, Greece

Asking the wine seller is a good start when you are faced with rows of daunting bottles

selecting wine

One of the easiest ways to buy a bottle of wine for tonight's supper or next week's family dinner is to buy the wine you enjoyed last week. There's no risk, you know you liked it, and it will probably go reasonably well with whatever is on the menu. But just before you reach for that same bottle, think again. If you are in a big supermarket, you probably have around 800 wines in front of you. That's 800 different combinations of flavor, region, and grape variety. Even if you drink a bottle of wine every night, and you have an endless supply of money, it would take over two years to try them all. So why waste one of those occasions by buying the same wine you drank last week?

Everyone has their favorites and we should rejoice in coming back to familiar flavors, but one of the great pleasures of buying and tasting wine is that each one is different. It has come from a different place, it has been made in a different way, and its flavors are resolutely different.

But how should you go about selecting a different wine? You could take a note of the grape variety of the bottle that you enjoyed. If it was a Cabernet Sauvignon from California, then why not try the same grape from Chile, or Australia, or perhaps France? Try following the flavors of a grape around the world. Or, take an in-depth look at the wines from one country. Start in Spain and try Rioja, Navarra, Ribera del Duero, and Penedès.

Shopping

One of the best things about buying from a supermarket is that there is no one to pressure you into buying something too expensive. It is easy to find something within your budget and to escape through the checkout without anyone raising an eyebrow. But in general there is no one to ask about wine. If you read the back-label, you will learn a little, but it is not the same as finding out about how it tastes.

A dedicated wine store is completely different. Here the staff will probably have a lot of experience in wine and they are keen to sell you something good. They probably will have tasted most of the wines they stock, and their job is not to sell you the most expensive one. They want to sell you the wine that is right for you, and they hope you will come back next week so they can do it all over again. There will probably be wines available to taste, so you can see if you like them. These tasting wines will not be the most expensive wine, but they are unlikely to be the the cheapest either, so you can start to get a feel for what is in their range.

Wine tastings

Regular wine tastings might be held at that dedicated wine store. For a small sum, you can taste dozens of wines so you can really grow to appreciate the flavors from around the world. Get on their mailing list so you can also find out about visiting winemakers and attending gourmet dinners and other events that will open up the world of wine to you. One of the best ways to learn about wine is to get together with a group of friends and meet regularly to share bottles. If you can do this in your own neighborhood, preferably within walking distance, you will not only be able to taste the wines, but also to drink and enjoy them.

An organized food and wine matching tasting, at Neil Ellis Wines, Stellenbosch

The best clubs are made up of no more than 16 members. That is because you will get around 16 tasting samples from each bottle, and for most people this is enough guests to have in their home. One person should be appointed to arrange the next tasting. His or her job is to read up about a region and then select some wines to show the diversity within that region. The wines are tasted seriously, and then probably enjoyed over a supper.

It sounds boring, but by the time you get home you will have forgotten which of those wines you liked best. I have met many people in front of wine shelves in stores as they puzzle over the labels—did the wine they liked have a green label or was it yellow? Was it Cabernet Franc or Carmenère? If you have not written it down, you will forget. We all do. Start a notebook and write down what you taste and whether you liked it.

Selecting wine in a restaurant

The same rules apply in restaurants as they do in stores. The easy way is always to choose the same wine, to stay in the comfort zone of price and familiarity, but you may do better if you ask the wine waiter for advice. He knows the menu and what will really complement the food. He might also be able to give you suggestions to cope with a table where some people are eating fish and the others venison. A wine waiter or sommelier will always try to talk up sales, but if you give him a price limit he should come up with three suggestions—low, middle, and high price.

If there is nobody to ask, then it is worth looking at lesser-known regions for the real bargains. The wine list will probably make bigger profits on the well-known, reliable wines, but if you try some of the less-known wines, you may get more flavor for your money.

If two of you have chosen wildly different dishes, there may not be a compromise wine. In this case you could select wine by the glass, so long as the restaurant has a regular turnover or one of those clever inert gas systems that keeps opened bottles fresh.

Cork or screwcap?

A few years ago all wine bottles were sealed with a cork, apart from the real cheap ones with a screwcap. Then brightly colored plastic stoppers arrived, followed by a whole array of different stoppers, agglomerates, specially treated agglomerates, and up-market screwcaps, which often go by the brand name of Stelvin. Why the change? Toward the end of the twentieth century, the demand for cork had grown so high that the whole industry was under strain. When that happened, standards dropped and the incidence of "cork taint" grew to alarming proportions. At one point it was reckoned that around one bottle in every case of twelve was affected by a musty, corky taste that made the wine undrinkable. That was the trigger for alternatives to move into the market.

Now the cork industry has improved its standards and the incidence of cork taint has subsided, but we still have the array of closures, in particular the screwcap which has shown itself to be particularly good for fresh-tasting white wines, some reds such as New World Pinot Noir, and young reds that do not require aging.

Will it keep?

One of the first questions many people ask about wine is whether it will keep. There seems to be a built-in assumption that wine will improve if you lay it down and leave it for a couple of years. For the vast majority of wine on the shelves, this is wrong. Most wine is made to be drinkable when you buy it. Its fresh fruity flavors are there, just waiting for you to enjoy. Some wines, particularly reds, do need time to develop and age, but the trick is to discover which ones they are. The best way to find out is to ask the person you buy it from. Otherwise use this rule:

Wines costing **less than $20** are unlikely to improve much with age, although they will not come to any harm if you keep them for a year or so.

Wines costing **between $20 and $40** are likely to develop more interesting flavors with a little age, say two to three years.

Wines costing **more than $40** might well appreciate two or more years of age, perhaps even a decade or so.

As an added guide, the more tannin a grape variety has, the more likely it will develop with age. Cabernet Sauvignon, Nebbiolo, and serious Shiraz wines need more age than, say, a New World Pinot. But good red Burgundy also needs age. Check the stopper. If there is a screwcap, then the producer is probably not expecting you to lay it down for more than a year.

Whatever its age, old wine is unlikely to go off. It certainly will not harm you, but it may have lost some of the fruit character that the winemaker intended to be there. On the other hand, it may have evolved into a glorious, complex wine. Just pull the cork and try it. One of the best ways to find out how a wine ages is to buy a dozen bottles. Keep them in a safe place and from time to time open one of the bottles to enjoy with supper. Over the months and years you will get to know the flavors and how they evolve. Write down your thoughts and keep your notes safe. Before you have finished that case of wine, buy another, the same or something different. Pretty soon you have a cellar, enjoying the changing flavors of wine as they age.

Barrel cellar, Jarnac, France

storing and serving wine

The best place to keep your wine is in a wine cellar, at a constant temperature between 40°F and 50°F, in the dark with no vibration. The bottles should be horizontal or angled so that the cork (if there is one) is kept moist. But since most of us do not have cellars, then the best alternative is a north-facing room, a cupboard away from direct heat, or even a corner in an insulated garage. Keep a thermometer near your wine, preferably one of those maximum and minimum ones that will tell you whether your chosen place varies a lot in temperature. If it does, then try to insulate around the rack, to keep temperature fluctuations as little as possible. A wine rack is ideal and can be used for bottles with all kinds of stoppers, but if the bottle has a screwcap there is no need to keep it horizontal.

Glasses

Good wine should taste the same no matter whether it arrives in a plastic cup or a fine glass—but it does not. After being in the bottle for several months or years, wine needs space and air to open up in the glass, so it is worthwhile investing in a good set of glasses. They should be made of clear glass, tulip-shaped, wider at the bowl than at the rim, and with stems, so you can hold the glass without touching the bowl of the glass. Holding the bowl warms up the wine, and prevents you from seeing the glorious deep, rich colors in the wine. Fill the glass no more than half-full to allow the wine room to breathe and space for you to swirl it around to release the aromas.

In a perfect world, glasses should be washed by hand and rinsed in clear water before being polished dry with a clean linen cloth. In reality, dishwashers are fine, but rinse-aid residue on the glass can reduce the bubbles in sparkling wines.

Store glasses upright. Inverting them traps a pocket of air which could taint the wine

Serving temperatures

The general rule for serving wine is that white wines should be chilled and red wines should be served at room temperature, but this is far too general. For a start, room temperature doesn't mean the temperature of your kitchen when you have been cooking all day, nor does it mean the living room, close to a radiator or a roaring fire.

The ideal serving temperature for most red wines is between 50°F and 64°F, depending on the amount of tannin in the wine. Light, fruity wines with little tannin, such as a Chilean Pinot Noir or a generic Beaujolais, should be served chilled, between 50°F and 54°F. Wines with more body and tannin, such as a Merlot or Chianti, should be served between 57°F and 63°F, while dense tannic wines such as a Barolo or a top-quality Cabernet Sauvignon can tolerate temperatures of 59°F to 64°F.

Red wine should not be served too warm because it muddles the flavors and makes the wine taste soupy. It is always far better to serve it slightly too cold than slightly too warm. You can always pour just a little into the glass and hold the glass to warm it with the palm of your hand.

Decanters

We all have a collection of decanters sitting in a cupboard gathering dust. Does anyone still use them? You should. If a wine has been in the bottle for several years, two things may have happened. It may have a deposit, which means that some of the tannin and coloring in the wine has gathered at the bottom of the bottle. This is not harmful, but it can make the wine cloudy and bitter-tasting unless you pour the liquid off first. The wine might also have "closed up" in the bottle. This is not as drastic as it sounds, but as a natural product, the flavors and aromas knit together so that they do not instantly appear when the cork is pulled. Allowing the wine to "breathe" for an hour before serving means that these flavors come to the fore, to be enjoyed.

To decant off a sediment, allow the wine to stand up for a couple of days in advance of opening. Then open the bottle and, with a strong light behind the neck of the bottle, pour the wine into a clean decanter in one clean, smooth motion. Stop when the sediment appears in the neck of the bottle. You can then rinse out the bottle and pour the wine back into it if you prefer.

To give the wine some air, the process is just the same. In both cases, you don't actually need a proper decanter. A large pitcher works just as well, but it is essential that it is clean and taint-free to avoid tainting the wine.

The most effective way to taste wine uses all the senses

how to taste

This must surely be the easiest part of wine drinking? It is, but like all things, the more you put into it, the more you get out. For a start, the overall taste of a wine is a complex combination of taste and smell. The nose is equally, if not more, important to the overall appreciation of flavor as the tongue. The palate itself can only distinguish between sweetness, acidity, bitterness, salt, and a savoriness known as umami. The remaining flavors—the hints of cherries, raspberries, chocolate, and spice—come from the olfactory area of the nose, which picks up these signals from molecules swept up into the nasal cavity. If you swirl the wine around in the glass and then sniff, you will find these aromas. When the wine is in the mouth, if you "chew" it or slurp some air in—all wine tasters slurp quite dreadfully—these molecules will register as flavors in your brain.

Just remember how you used to drink something horrid as a child. You held your nose. If you don't use your nose in wine tasting, you are missing most of the fun. Tannin can register in the mouth. It is the drying, bitter effect on the surface of the mouth and is the reason many people say they dislike red wine. Tannin softens as the wine ages and is a vital part of quality red wine. You can also detect alcohol in the mouth, as warmth on the back of the palate.

Tasting words

At your first wine tasting, you will probably come across a person who describes a wine like this: "Crisp and floral with raspberry juiciness, layers of chocolate and spice with a hot finish," and all you can taste is—well, wine. Have you got it wrong? Are your tastebuds defective? No and no.

Wine tasting takes practice and so does its vocabulary. Imagine trying to explain the taste of a lamb chop to someone who has never tasted one. It is difficult. The best way to build your own vocabulary is to enjoy life with your nose open. Smell black currants straight from the garden, still warm with sunshine, and then think of Cabernet Sauvignon. Do not just eat that berry compote, get your nose in there and smell it. Then think of Shiraz. Go for a walk after it has rained and smell the scent of the earth. Think about that when you next open a bottle of good Pinot Noir. Stand next to the road when they are laying a new surface and sniff deeply. Then go home and open a bottle of Pinotage. All these experiences will help you build up your own vocabulary. And if you think raspberries when the next guy thinks strawberries, you are both right. Writing tasting notes is just finding a peg to hang a flavor on. Whatever notes you take, they are your notes, no one else's.

A wine fair in Paris—there are annual wine fairs internationally.
These are great events to get you into the world of wine

Bresaola and apple shavings on rye bread at a wine tasting

food and wine

Good with food. These three words appear on more wine labels than you can count. But what kind of food?

As with all things in life there are no absolute rules, but there are certain affinities between food and wine that will help you find the best combinations.

Think about weight—not the amount of food on the plate but the weight and texture of the food in your mouth. Light foods such as salads and plain broiled fish need light wines to accompany them, and as the food choices become heavier—roast chicken, fish dishes with sauce—you need wines with more weight and texture to balance them. With seriously weighty foods such as roast beef, game, and winter casseroles, a hefty, full-flavored wine is called for. Acidity is important too. Tomato-rich dishes need a wine with some acidity to balance, while tannic wines need some meat or cheese to round out the effect.

at-a-glance food pairings

Food	Sauce or flavoring	Wine suggestion
Broiled fish	Lemon, butter, and herbs	Beaujolais, Dolcetto d'Alba
Fish pie	A mix of fish in a creamy sauce	Chilean Pinot Noir, young Rioja
Roast chicken	Roasted with herbs, served cold with salad	Côtes du Rhone, Oregon Pinot Noir
Roast chicken	Hot, with sauces, gravy, and vegetables	Minervois, Chilean Merlot
Chicken casserole	Red wine sauce	California Central Coast Cabernet, Bourgogne Rouge
Duck	Plain roasted or broiled	Crozes-Hermitage, Argentinian Malbec
Duck	Hot, with a fruit-based sauce	Barossa Shiraz, Central Coast Syrah
Lamb	Roasted	St Emilion, Beaune
Lamb	Casserole	Corbières, Navarra
Pheasant, Grouse	Casserole	Châteauneuf-du-Pape, California Zinfandel

Food	Sauce or flavoring	Wine suggestion
Beef	Roasted, still pink, served cold	Rioja Reserva, New York State Merlot
Beef	Roasted, served hot with a rich sauce	Napa Cabernet, South African Pinotage
Beef steak	Broiled	Barolo, McLaren Vale Shiraz
Pork	Roasted, with herbs	Médoc, Douro
Pasta	Tomato-based sauce	Argentinian Bonarda, Rosso Conero
Hard cheeses	Cheddar, Parmesan, Manchego	Ribera del Duero, California Merlot, Rioja Gran Reserve
Soft cheeses	Camembert, Chaource, Epoisses	Burgundy, young New World Shiraz
Blue cheese	Stilton	Port, Zinfandel
Chocolate	Desserts	California Cabernet, Port, Banyuls

glossary

Acidity	Naturally present in grapes, acidity gives freshness to a wine and helps it age. Too much can make the wine taste sharp.
Aging	Aging a red wine in tank, cask, or bottle helps soften tannins and allows complexity to develop. Too much aging can cause a wine to lose its fruit flavors. Some white wines also develop complexity with age such as white Burgundys and sweet wines.
Barrel/barrique	Barrique is the name for a 50 gallon barrel traditionally used in France. Usually made of French oak, barriques are used in many wineries around the world for aging and sometimes for fermenting wine.
Biodynamic	This is a holistic approach to viticulture and winemaking, taking account of the forces of the moon and the energy of the earth.
Blending and cépage	A wine may be made of several different grape varieties all of which ripen at different times. Once the wines have been made they will be blended to give a more complex flavor. The cépage is the composition of the blend.
Canopy	The growth of the leaves, stems, and fruit above ground.
Claret	The term used in England for red wine from Bordeaux.
Cold soak	A technique sometimes used before fermentation to allow fruity flavors to develop.
Cru	French for a single vineyard, often used to signify specific quality.
Fermentation	A process where yeast transforms grape sugars into alcohol.
Fortification	A winemaking process in which spirit is added to a wine to increase the alcohol and/or stop fermentation.
Hybrid	A vine created from the normal wine-producing vine *Vitis vinifera* with another vine species. This is usually done to combine desirable characteristics in the resulting plant.
Maceration	A period of steeping the grapes in the fermenting liquid, either before or after fermentation.

Malolactic fermentation	A secondary fermentation, after the alcoholic fermentation which transforms harsh malic acid to softer lactic acids. Almost all red wines and some whites go through this process.
Meritage	A term used in North America for a traditional Bordeaux blend of grapes.
Microclimate	The immediate area around a vine which has an affect on the way it grows.
Oak	The most common wood used for wine casks. It can come from various countries, each one has a slightly different effect. American oak is distinctively different.
Organic	The basic concept of organic is that chemical pesticides and fertilizers are banned, however the practice is tied up in legislation which does not permit agrochemicals but does allow sprays such as sulpur and copper. Actual regulations vary across the world but are generally of a good standard.
Phenolics	The compounds found in the skins, pips and stalks of grapes which transfer to the wine adding structure, color, and flavor, particularly in red wines.
Sulfur	A naturally occurring element which acts as a natural disinfectant, preventing microbial spoilage. Commonly used in the wine and food industries.
Tannin	Derived from the grape skins and pips, tannins form the backbone of a wine and soften during aging.
Terroir	French term for the natural environment of a vineyard site, encompassing soil, mesoclimate, and microclimate.
Vintage	The actual year of production. It has no particular quality connotations.
Yeast	The yeast *Saccharomyces cerevisiae* is naturally found on grape skins in vineyards around the world. This ferments sugars into alcohol. Specific strains of this yeast may be cultured on an industrial scale and used to produce reliable fermentations to generate specific flavors.
Yield	The amount of fruit a vine can produce—if yield is restricted the flavors in the grapes are more concentrated. An optimum crop is one which is commercially viable yet produces flavorful grapes.

CANADA

Vancouver

Washington

Oregon

San Fransisco

California

Los Angeles

UNITED STATES

Toronto

New York State

New York

Washington D.C.

Southwest U.S. & Mexico

Houston

North America

Despite the relatively recent appearance of American wine on worldwide markets, grape growing and winemaking in America are hardly new. The early settlers on the eastern seaboard found wild vines in their new land, and since then farmers have sought the right vines and conditions for their successful cultivation.

Now the United States is the fourth-largest wine producer in the world—after France, Italy, and Spain—and wine is made in each of its 50 states; although, for now at least, Alaska has to rely on grapes produced outside its own state boundary. Ninety percent of America's production is in California, and most of that volume comes from the Central Valley. The real jewels in California's wine industry are from pockets of vineyards scattered down its coastline and along the foothills of its mountains.

Less important in terms of volume is Washington state, although its contribution to overall quality is notable, with a range of Cabernets, Malbecs, and Merlots grown in its frost-prone but warm climate. Cool-climate Oregon is dominated by soft, elegant Pinot Noirs that can challenge many Pinots from around the world.

In the Southwest, Texas is seeing a resurgence in grape growing, while over the border, the centuries-old Mexican wine industry is starting to expand. Recent years have seen a renaissance of viticulture in New York state, with quality Merlot and Cabernet Franc replacing old hybrid vines in this marginal climate. Canada's cold winters mean that much of its winemaking effort has been focused on ice wine (harvested in the depths of winter), but red-grape planting is increasing quickly, especially in the warm, sunny vineyards of British Columbia.

① Mendocino & Lake County
② Sonoma
③ Napa
④ Central Valley
⑤ North Central Coast
⑥ South Central Coast

CALIFORNIA

The Pacific Ocean and large
bays serve as tempering
influences to most California
wine regions, providing cool
winds and fog that balance
the heat and sunshine.
Although drought can be a
hazard, most regions receive
24–45 inches of rain annually.

PACIFIC OCEAN

NEVADA

CALIFORNIA

San Francisco

Santa Cruz

Fresno

Santa Maria

Los Angeles

California

California is blessed with a climate and a range of vineyards that can produce wines that range from good value, easy-drinking styles to handcrafted icons that can stand alongside some of the best wines in the world. By latitude alone, California equates to the warmer parts of southern Europe, but the cold Pacific Ocean has a dramatic effect on the climate, chilling the air and creating fogs that roll in from the coast, spreading through gaps in the hills into inland valleys and keeping temperatures down until the sun can burn them off.

Distance from the ocean is an important factor in determining the climate, but so is the range of hills, some of which protect the vineyards, while others act like funnels, sucking in cold air even as far away as 75 miles from the coast.

Rain falls mainly in winter months, so summers are warm and long, allowing a long ripening period in fall. Cabernet Sauvignon, Merlot, and Zinfandel have traditionally been planted in all regions, but now cooler sites have been identified for Pinot Noir, while Syrah looks set to find its niche, too.

Mendocino &
Lake County

Rapidly gaining recognition as a place to grow cool-climate grapes, Mendocino is California's northernmost wine-producing region. Closest to the Pacific and its attendant cooling fogs, this is most suited to white grapes, although Pinot Noir is developing well. Farther inland, the warmth of Redwood Valley ripens Zinfandel varieties, and Lake County benefits from warm days, tempered by cool mountain air at night. Pinot Noir, Merlot, and Cabernet Franc are important here.

CALIFORNIA

Mendocino

Ukiah

Lake

The family-run Navarro Vineyards in Anderson Valley have been producing wine since 1974

① Edmeades Zinfandel, Mendocino County

Grapes for this wine come from rocky vineyards on the Mendocino Ridge and in Redwood Valley, where old vines yield concentrated flavors of black cherries and licorice, backed by crisp acidity and mellowed by toasty, spicy oak.

Food pairings: Grilled chicken with barbecue sauce
Vintage years: 2006, 2005, 2001

② Steele DuPratt Zinfandel, Mendocino

Located in Lake County, sourcing fruit from its own vineyards and surrounding areas, this wine is made from 80-year-old vines planted on the Mendocino Ridge. It provides deep-flavored wild berry and cherry fruit and spice with muscular tannins and a peppery finish.

Food pairings: Seared rib-eye steak
Vintage years: 2006, 2004, 2001

④ Bonterra Zinfandel, Mendocino County

Bonterra wines are made with utmost care, using organically grown grapes and absolute respect for the environment. This Zinfandel is packed with raspberry and bramble fruit aromas, with white pepper, cedar spice, and mature, silky tannins.

Food pairings: Pasta dishes with beef
Vintage years: 2006, 2005, 2004

③ Goldeneye Pinot Noir, Anderson Valley

Dan and Margaret Duckhorn, of Napa Valley fame, specialize in Pinot Noir here. The wine has the flavor of bright strawberries backed by dark cherries, with nutmeg and vanilla oak. The second label, Migration, is lighter and fresher.

Food pairings: Broiled salmon
Vintage years: 2005, 2004, 2002

⑤ Navarro Vineyards Pinot Noir, Anderson Valley

White wines may be the main event at this small producer, but this Pinot Noir has wonderful black cherry and wild berry fruit aromas, notes of hazelnut and spice, with fine-grained silky tannins and a focused finish.

Food pairings: Pan-roasted chicken
Vintage years: 2006, 2004, 2002

① ❙ ② ❙❙ ③ ❙❙❙ ④ ❙ ⑤ ❙❙

Sonoma

North of San Francisco Bay, Sonoma is one of California's most important wine regions. Vineyards were established here in the mid-nineteenth century and have spread throughout this geographically and climatically diverse region. As in most of California, fog through gaps in the hills and along valleys determines the local climate. Here Russian River produces elegant Pinot Noirs and good Zinfandels, which benefit from longer ripening in the cool climate. Farther north, the inland warmth of Alexander Valley gives Zinfandels and Cabernets great depth and character.

CALIFORNIA

An old Zinfandel vine grows in Ravenswood Winery, Sonoma County

1 Marimar Torres, Don Miguel Vineyard Pinot Noir, Russian River

Marimar Torres of the Catalan Torres wine-producing family specializes in Chardonnay and Pinot Noir wines of top quality. High-density, low-yielding, organic vineyards produce a firm, structured Pinot with wild berry and cherry fruit, herbs, and spice on the finish.

Food pairings: Seared tuna medallions with chanterelles
Vintage years: 2005, 2004, 2001

2 Dry Creek Vineyards, Old Vine Zinfandel, Sonoma County

This family-owned vineyard produces lush bramble-soaked wines from 80-year-old Zinfandel vines. A lift of acidity is added by 10% Petite Sirah, and 18 months in oak adds complexity and spice. Dense, rich-tasting, and concentrated, with capacity to age.

Food pairings: Simple pasta dishes with beef or pizza
Vintage years: 2006, 2005, 2003

4 Rodney Strong Vineyards, Symmetry, Alexander Valley

The fine blend of Cabernet Sauvignon, Merlot, Malbec, and Petit Verdot from mountain and hillside vineyards in Alexander Valley produces a deep-flavored, blackberry, cassis, and plum fruit wine, with chocolate and spice notes and smooth ripe tannins.

Food pairings: Braised beef casserole with a touch of chile
Vintage years: 2005, 2004, 2001

3 Flowers Camp Meeting Ridge, Pinot Noir, Sonoma Coast

The combination of quality Pinot Noir grapes from these high-altitude vineyards with Burgundian techniques of native yeast fermentation and punch-down yield a wine with red currant and raspberry fruit, white pepper, and a vanilla-edged finish.

Food pairings: Lamb chops
Vintage years: 2005, 2004, 2002

5 Paul Hobbs, Pinot Noir, Russian River Valley

Paul Hobbs sets the pace for change in Chile and Argentina as well as making benchmark wines in Sonoma. Native yeast gives structured, complex wines, capable of aging. This Pinot has deep plum and cherry fruit flavors and firm, smooth tannins.

Food pairings: Seared tuna or salmon
Vintage years: 2006, 2005, 2004

6 Ravenswood, Zinfandel, Sonoma County

Old Zinfandel vines, mainly from Dry Creek and Sonoma Valley, provide extra dimension and muscular balance. A splash of Carignane and Petite Sirah balances the flavors of raspberries and blackberries with warm cinnamon and soft vanilla oak.

Food pairings: Grilled ribs glazed with ginger and soy sauce
Vintage years: 2006, 2005, 2004

7 Seghesio Home Ranch Zinfandel, Alexander Valley

The Seghesio family recently cut back production to focus on fruit from their own vines. This old vineyard, in the warmth of the Alexander Valley, ripens Zinfandel perfectly, giving spicy cherry and blackberry fruit and a rich, lingering finish.

Food pairings: Beef, game, and pasta dishes
Vintage years: 2006, 2005, 2004

9 Williams Selyem, Hirsch Vineyard Pinot Noir, Sonoma Coast

Hirsch Vineyard—on a rugged mountain ridge, close to the ocean, but above the fogline—receives plenty of sunshine. That shows in the wine, which has vibrant, expansive, cherry fruit flavors and creamy tannins, with herbs and spice on the finish.

Food pairings: Broiled duck breast
Vintage years: 2006, 2004, 2001

8 St Francis, Cabernet Sauvignon Wild Oak, Sonoma County

This medium-sized winery produces good, accessible quality. Grapes from small, mountainous vineyards result in impressive, dense wine with black currant dusted with spice and an integrated finish.

Food pairings: Steak with peppercorn sauce
Vintage years: 2006, 2005, 2004

10 J. Rochioli, Pinot Noir, Russian River Valley

Iconic and expensive wines come from this meticulous 161-acre farm. This Pinot Noir has ripe and expressive red berry and black cherry flavors, a dusting of wild herbs, and a touch of spice on the finish with silky, minerally tannins that will age well.

Food pairings: Broiled red meats or salmon
Vintage years: 2005, 2004, 2003

6 ❘   7 ❘❘❘   8 ❘❘   9 ❘❘❘❘❘ 10 ❘❘❘❘❘

American oak is intensely flavored and provides deep, powerful reds

Napa & Carneros

Originally planted in the 1800s, Napa Valley is the standard bearer for Californian wines around the world. The word Napa means "plenty," and it refers to the fertile valley-floor soils and the gentle climate. Reds do exceptionally well here, particularly Cabernets, although Merlot and even Zinfandel produce intensely flavored wines. Some of the best vineyards are now on slopes at higher altitudes, where cooler temperatures create more complexity in the wine. The cool Carneros district, south of Napa, is a top area for elegant Pinot Noir, with Merlot and even Syrah showing promise.

Beringer Vineyards, long established in Napa, produce top-quality Private Reserve Cabernets

① Viader Estate, Napa Valley

Tiny quantities of top wines come from Viader in the Howell Mountain foothills. This sleek, elegant blend of Cabernet Sauvignon and Cabernet Franc is aged 24 months in French oak and shows spicy currant and blackberry fruit, with seamlessly integrated oak.

Food pairings: Oven-roasted red meats such as prime rib
Vintage years: 2003, 2001, 2000

② Beringer, Founder's Estate Merlot, Napa Valley

Beringer is one of Napa's long-established names. Age-worthy Private Reserve Cabernets are among Napa's best, but this approachable, affordable Merlot is full of appealing blackberry flavors with soft tannins and a satisfying finish.

Food pairings: Steak au poivre
Vintage years: 2006, 2005, 2004

④ Frog's Leap, Zinfandel, Napa Valley

A serious winery despite the frog references. Organic, dry-farming gives concentrated, structured wines. The Zinfandel is more complex and less of a monster than it used to be and has wild berry and fresh fruit flavors with layers of spice.

Food pairings: Jalapeño-stuffed pork loin
Vintage years: 2006, 2004, 1999

③ Clos du Val, Cabernet Sauvignon, Napa Valley

Elegant Cabernets with a French accent at this 150-acre estate at the heart of Napa's Stags Leap District. Cofounder Bernard Portet makes dense, dusty, earthy wines, with blackberry and plummy fruit in a structure of firm, ripe tannins. Needs time.

Food pairings: Beef tenderloin with roasted vegetables
Vintage years: 2003, 2001, 1997

⑤ Chateau Montelena, Cabernet Sauvignon, Napa Valley

This historic property from the 1880s is famed for its Cabernet-based estate wines, which are plush, concentrated, and long-lived. This Cabernet has more tannins, but still exudes generous, fleshy, black currant fruit. It has a focused, elegant finish.

Food pairings: Leg of lamb with rosemary and garlic
Vintage years: 2005, 2003, 2001

6 Saintsbury, Pinot Noir, Carneros

Cool breezes from San Pablo Bay and clay-loam soils of Carneros create the right conditions for great Pinot Noir. New Dijon clones and low yields produce accessible, affordable wines with clear raspberry fruit, with simple spice and gentle tannins.

Food pairings: Broiled sea bass with mushrooms and couscous
Vintage years: 2006, 2003, 2001

7 Opus One, Napa Valley

This iconic joint venture between old-world Bordeaux and new-world California has always been a wine of power and complexity. A Cabernet-dominated blend, it needs time to reveal its full splendor of blackberry and black cherry fruit with vanilla, peppercorns, and chocolate.

Food pairings: Beef tenderloin with a wild mushroom sauce
Vintage years: 2004, 2001, 1999

9 Stag's Leap Wine Cellars, S.L.V. Cabernet Sauvignon, Napa Valley

Forever famous for its success against top Bordeaux three decades ago, this property still makes excellent, expensive wines. This Cabernet Reserve has rich flavors of chocolate, rosemary, and vanilla. It will build and develop for 10 years.

Food pairings: Oven-roasted fillet of beef with mushrooms
Vintage years: 2001, 2000, 1997

8 Shafer, Relentless, Napa Valley

High quality is found across the range in Stags Leap District. Relentless, a field blend of Syrah and Petite Sirah and aged 30 months in French oak, is robust and full of blackberry and blueberry flavors, rolled up in complex, meaty savoriness and silky tannins.

Food pairings: Slow-roasted pork with bacon and spiced applesauce
Vintage years: 2005, 2003, 2000

10 Araujo, Cabernet Sauvignon Eisele Vineyard, Napa Valley

Iconic, expensive, and deservedly so. From the Eisele Vineyard in the northeastern part of Napa, this wine is tight and well-structured, with ripe cherry and floral fruit; spicy, toasty oak; and a long, persistent finish.

Food pairings: Standing rib roast
Vintage years: 2004, 2000, 1999

6 ▮▮▮   7 ▮▮▮▮▮   8 ▮▮▮▮▮   9 ▮▮▮▮▮   10 ▮▮▮▮▮

11 Newton, Unfiltered Cabernet Sauvignon, Napa Valley

A most spectacular estate, with vineyards on mountainous slopes. Meticulous care produces top-quality wines. Natural yeast fermentation and no filtration make these wines intense, focused, and complex, with fleshy, plummy fruit and a structured finish.

Food pairings: Beef Wellington
Vintage years: 2005, 2000, 1999

12 Dominus Estate, Napa Valley

Owned by Christian Moueix, part of the dynasty responsible for Ch. Pétrus, Dominus makes elegant wines with clear classic style. Concentrated, with ripe currant and cedary fruit, Dominus needs years to emerge from its structure. Napanook is the more affordable second wine.

Food pairings: Beef tenderloin with chanterelles
Vintage years: 2002, 2000, 1995.

14 Joseph Phelps, Cabernet Sauvignon, Napa Valley

Made by a master of Cabernet Sauvignon, this has ripe, elegant, defined fruit with touches of cinnamon, licorice, and caramel, balanced by supple tannins. Even more intense is top wine Insignia, a Cabernet-dominated blend that can age for over a decade.

Food pairings: Herb-stuffed roast goose
Vintage years: 2002, 2001, 1999

13 Duckhorn, Estate Grown Merlot, Napa Valley

Merlot is the main focus here, but there is excellent Cabernet too. This Estate Merlot comes from the best alluvial soils in Napa Valley and offers aromas of plum, vanilla, and spice with blackberry, tobacco, and mocha notes across the structured palate.

Food pairings: Peking duck pancakes with plum sauce
Vintage years: 2005, 2004, 2001

15 Pine Ridge, Cabernet Sauvignon, Napa Valley

Pine Ridge owns several vineyards across Napa, but this flagship Cabernet comes from the steep hillsides of Stags Leap District. Low yields produce intense wines with black cherry, tobacco, chocolate, and clove notes, and a rich structured finish.

Food pairings: Confit shoulder of lamb
Vintage years: 2005, 2003, 2002

16 Heitz, Cabernet Sauvignon Bella Oaks, Napa Valley

Martha's Vineyard Cabernet is the legend of the Napa for its deep-flavored minty style, but other wines from the Heitz cellars deserve attention. Bella Oaks Cabernet has intense red currant and black cherry fruit with complexity and a long, structured finish.

Food pairings: Boeuf bourguignon with mushrooms and caramelized onions
Vintage years: 2003, 2001, 1997

17 Cakebread Cellars, Cabernet Sauvignon, Napa Valley

Using grapes from warm Calistoga in the north down to the cool of Carneros Cakebread creates complexity and retains acidity. The wine has ripe fig, blackberry, and cassis aromas; a rich textured palate with coffee and chocolate notes; and a savory finish.

Food pairings: Rib-eye roast
Vintage years: 2002, 2001, 2000

19 Stonehedge Winery Reserve Cabernet Sauvignon, Napa Valley

Made from grapes grown on a rocky hillside in the Atlas Peak district, this wine is loaded with flavors of currants and sweet cherries. Big and powerful with ripe tannins and a long finish.

Food pairings: Roast chicken with apricot stuffing
Vintage years: 2005

18 Robert Mondavi, Cabernet Sauvignon, Napa Valley

Now owned by a multinational company, the top-level Mondavi wines still retain their flagship status. This shines with sleek elegance, showing blackberry and cassis aromas, overlaid with black olive flavors and dark chocolate, with smooth, fine-grained tannins.

Food pairings: Braised beef short ribs
Vintage years: 2005, 2003, 2001

20 Hess Collection, Cabernet Sauvignon, Mount Vedeer, Napa Valley

Hess owns wine interests around the world, all producing quality wines. Single-vineyard wines from here show impressive depth, while the collection range provides round, well-defined flavors.

Food pairings: Pot-roasted chicken with smoked bacon
Vintage years: 2004, 2002, 2001

Wild mustard grows at the Robert Mondavi winery in Napa Valley

North Central Coast

In the early 1800s the San Francisco Bay area used to be a very important wine region, but now urban sprawl has taken over. To the east of San Francisco, Livermore Valley produces good Cabernets and Petite Sirah; while to the south, the Santa Cruz Mountains are home to some of California's most distinctive producers such as Ridge, David Bruce, and Bonny Doon. Here, old vines and warm sunshine above the Pacific fogline combine to produce quality Zinfandel, Cabernet, and Rhône varietals. Farther south vineyards of Monterey stretch southeast into the Salinas Valleya and into the Santa Lucia Highlands.

Ridge Vineyards in the Santa Cruz Mountains

1 Cycles Gladiator, Syrah, Central Coast

This comes from the same people who make estate wines from Santa Lucia Highlands under the Hahn Estates label. Enjoy the aromatic fruit of their SLH Pinot Noir at a price, but for sheer easy drinking and exuberant fruit, Cycles Gladiator has it all.

Food pairings: Seared strip steak in a crunchy sourdough sandwich
Vintage years: 2007, 2006

2 Bernardus, Marinus, Carmel Valley

Dense planting and the high altitude of the Carmel Valley lead to long, slow ripening and intense flavors in this Bordeaux-blend wine. Marinus 2003 is ripe, dense, and concentrated with blackberry and blueberry fruit combined with minerally, earthy notes and ripe, structuring tannins.

Food pairings: Broiled chicken with corn fritters
Vintage years: 2003, 2002, 2000

4 Concannon, Heritage Petite Sirah, Livermore Valley

East of San Francisco, behind a range of hills, the Livermore Valley is warm and windy. Petite Sirah ripens well and continues to make good wine here at Concannon, with big, bold red currant and plum fruit; spice; and sleek, supple tannins.

Food pairings: Beef or chicken pasta dishes
Vintage years: 2005, 2004, 2001

3 Heller Estate, Cabernet Sauvignon, Cachagua, Carmel Valley

Dry-farmed, organic vineyards at this 120-acre mountainous estate are planted with Bordeaux grapes and Pinot Noir. A substantial splash of Merlot rounds out the flavors, which are full of red berries, light spice, and juicy acidity.

Food pairings: Homemade hamburgers with tomato salsa
Vintage years: 2006, 2004, 2003

5 Ridge Vineyards, Ridge Monte Bello, Santa Cruz Mountains

Paul Draper at Ridge is a legend among winemakers. Deep, intense wines are the norm here, especially this top-quality, concentrated Monte Bello Cabernet-based icon, which takes a decade or more to come around.

Food pairings: Slow-cooked beef casserole with thyme
Vintage years: 2005, 2001, 1999

6 Morgan Winery, Twelve Clones Pinot Noir, Monterey County

This small producer gets its grapes mainly from the Santa Lucia Highlands, and Pinot Noir is a specialty here. This is approachable, refined with wild cherry and red currant notes, and a touch of spicy oak.

Food pairings: Chicken or vegetarian Provençale
Vintage years: 2006, 2005, 2004

7 Chalone, Pinot Noir, Chalone

This estate has its own AVA (American Viticultural Area) on a unique, sunny hilltop, 1,700 feet above the Salinas Valley. Recently planted new Pinot Noir clones are now producing silky, elegant wines with raspberry-scented fruit.

Food pairings: Seared wild salmon with sweet potato
Vintage years: 2006, 2005, 2004

9 Bonny Doon, Le Cigare Volant, Santa Cruz

Randall Grahm, the Rhône Ranger, continues to make quality wines with impressive flavors and great names. This Grenache-dominated Rhône blend of Mourvèdre, Carignane, and Cinsault has dense, chocolaty, red fruit aromas and sweet, spicy flavors.

Food pairings: Mexican-spiced red meat dishes
Vintage years: 2005, 2003, 2002

8 Calera, Pinot Noir Mount Harlan Cuvée, Central Coast

Calera is based on a limestone site, which, combined with high Mount Harlan, allows for long, slow ripening and excellent acidity in the wines. There are several single-vineyard Pinot Noirs. The Cuvée blend provides aromatic fruit with fine tannins.

Food pairings: Broiled lamb chops with rosemary glaze
Vintage years: 2006, 2005, 2004

10 David Bruce, Pinot Noir, Santa Cruz Mountains

Pinot Noir is the main focus in the 16 acres of vines overlooking the Pacific Ocean in the Santa Cruz Mountains. The flavors are intense with wild berry and cherry fruit, subtle toast and nutmeg, a touch of pepper, and velvety tannins.

Food pairings: Cumin-spiced chicken breast
Vintage years: 2005, 2004, 2002

6 ‖   7 | 8 ‖   9 ‖   10 ‖‖

Pinot Noir grapes are the main focus at David Bruce's vineyards in the Santa Cruz Mountains

South Central Coast

The stretch of land between Monterey and Los Angeles is marine-influenced in its soil, which has significant amounts of limestone, and in its climate, with mild winters and moderate summers. Protected by hills from the cooling effect of the coast, the warm vineyards of Paso Robles produce deep-flavored reds from Syrah, Zinfandel, and even Cabernet Sauvignon, while the cooler slopes of Santa Maria show that Pinot Noir can do well this far south. The surrounding Santa Ynez Valley is producing remarkable Rhône reds.

Bien Nacido Vineyards, Au Bon Climat, Santa Maria Valley

1 Cambria, Bench Break Pinot Noir, Santa Maria Valley

A large estate on benchland that rises up to meet the Pacific sea breezes. Pinot Noir and Syrah are good here, in particular a range of single clone Pinots. Bench Break comes from the most austere soil and shows minerally fruit and silky tannins.

Food pairings: Rack of lamb with thyme and rosemary
Vintage years: 2006, 2005, 2000

2 Justin, Isosceles, Paso Robles

Just 12 miles from the ocean, on south-facing slopes. Isosceles is Cabernet Sauvignon dominated with Cabernet Franc and Merlot, and aged 24 months in oak. It has ripe, juicy, dark red fruits; hints of mocha and cassis; and sleek, integrated tannins and ripe, structuring tannins.

Food pairings: Roast beef (with Yorkshire pudding for a real treat)
Vintage years: 2006, 2005, 2000

4 Qupé, Syrah, Central Coast

Single-vineyard Syrahs are the main focus at this producer in the Santa Maria Valley, but this Central Coast Syrah, sourced from a number of cool-climate sites across Santa Barbara County, offers peppery fruit, layers of licorice, and minerals at a very affordable price.

Food pairings: Moroccan-spiced lamb shank
Vintage years: 2006, 2005, 2002

3 Peachy Canyon, Westside Zinfandel, Paso Robles

A family-run winery where the focus is firmly on Zinfandel. Several single-vineyard wines show distinctive ripe berry fruit and spice. Westside blend provides tangy, wild berry fruit, plums, and toasty oak with white pepper and chocolate on the finish.

Food pairings: Grilled ribs
Vintage years: 2007, 2006, 2005

5 Au Bon Climat, Pinot Noir, Santa Maria Valley

Jim Clendenen produces several Pinots ranging from intense single-vineyard wines to affordable, enjoyable blends. This wine comes from the Bien Nacido Vineyards and has wild berry aromas, sage, and cherries on the palate with juicy acidity.

Food pairings: Broiled tuna steak with peppercorns
Vintage years: 2006, 2005, 2002

❻ Tablas Creek, Esprit de Beaucastel, Paso Robles 🛢

The Perrin family of Château de Beaucastel chose the hilly Las Tablas area because of its similarities to Châteauneuf-du-Pape. This is a typical southern Rhône blend, complex and layered with spicy plum flavors, and firm tannins.

Food pairings: Venison with currant sauce
Vintage years: 2006, 2005, 2004

❼ Sanford La Rinconada Vineyard, Pinot Noir, Santa Rita

Maritime breezes keep temperatures down in the Santa Rita Hills, allowing this Pinot to ripen slowly to a structured, rich-tasting wine, with layers of black cherry, plum, and an earthy quality adding complexity.

Food pairings: Broiled sea bass with herbs
Vintage years: 2006, 2004, 2001

❾ Zaca Mesa, Z Three, Santa Ynez Valley

Situated at 1,500 feet, facing the ocean breezes, Zaca Mesa has some of the oldest Syrah vines in the region. Z Three is an impressive, structured blend of Syrah, Mourvèdre, and Grenache with blackberry and raspberry fruit, layers of spice, and a bright, fruit-driven finish.

Food pairings: Peppered filet mignon
Vintage years: 2005, 2004, 2003

❽ Tantara, Pinot Noir, Santa Maria Valley

A small producer dedicated to making the very best Pinot Noir and Syrah. Using fruit from Bien Nacido Vineyards and other cool Central Coast areas, the wines are concentrated and elegant with well-focused blackberry and black cherry fruit; earthy, spicy notes; and supple tannins.

Food pairings: White fish or salmon in red wine
Vintage years: 2006, 2005, 2003

❿ Andrew Murray, Roasted Slope, Santa Ynez Valley

Rhône varietals are the focus here in the rolling hills. Five percent Viognier is interplanted among the Syrah, and low yields combined with old-style winemaking give a dense, concentrated wine with violets on the nose, black cherries, spices and ripe tannins.

Food pairings: Broiled beef tenderloin
Vintage years: 2005, 2001, 1999

Beautiful scenery surrounds the vineyards in Santa Ynez Valley

Central Valley & Sierra Foothills

Vast, hot, dry, and very fertile, California's Central Valley stretches about 300 miles from Sacramento to Bakersfield, an agricultural powerhouse fed by water from the Sierra Nevada ranges. Grapes thrive here and produce about 75 percent of California's wine. In the northern Sacramento River Valley, where there is still some maritime influence on the climate, old-vine Zinfandels produce dense, lush wines. To the east, in the cooler Sierra Foothills of Amador County, old Zinfandel vines and newly planted Barbera, Sangiovese, and Tempranillo are making their mark.

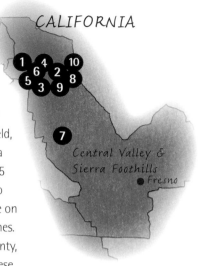

CALIFORNIA

1 4 10
6 2 8
5 3 9 7

Central Valley &
Sierra Foothills
● Fresno

Tempranillo grapes are used to make full-bodied red wine

1 Montevina, Terra d'Oro Zinfandel, Amador County

Zinfandel is the flagship variety at Montevina, grown on thin, rocky, decomposed granite soils in the Sierra Foothills. This Zinfandel is seasoned with Shenandoah spice, full of dark berry fruit, and rounding out with vanilla and cinnamon.

Food pairings: Pasta with Bolognese sauce
Vintage years: 2005, 2004, 2001

2 Christine Andrew, Tempranillo, Lodi

Ironstone is a long-established producer in the Sierra Foothills; Christine Andrew is the new premium label. The Tempranillo is deep purple in color, with aromas of ripe blackberries, violets, and olives. The palate has ripe fruit, minerals, and underlying spice with a complex, gentle finish.

Food pairings: Roast rack of lamb
Vintage years: 2006, 2005, 2004

4 Renwood, Old Vine Zinfandel, Amador County

Renwood Winery is in the foothills of the Sierra Nevada Mountains, surrounded by Zinfandel vineyards. Made from some of the best lots, this wine is full of berry-compote aromas, cinnamon spice with coffee bean notes, and soft tannins.

Food pairings: Italian eggplant dishes with parmigiana
Vintage years: 2007, 2006, 2005

3 Amador Foothill Winery, Clockspring Zinfandel, Shenandoah Valley

Lush plum and spice aromas with rich raspberry and plum fruit and black peppery spice in this Zinfandel from a certified organic vineyard on the warm slopes of Amador.

Food pairings: Pizza and anything on the barbecue
Vintage years: 2006, 2005, 2004

5 Michael David, Earthquake Syrah, Lodi

Fifth-generation growers Michael and David Phillips cultivate 500 acres of premium wine grapes in Lodi. Earthquake is the reserve level, and all the Earthquake wines have massive flavors. The Syrah is full of luscious cherry and red berry fruit, with toasty caramel oak.

Food pairings: Beef pasta dishes such as canneloni
Vintage years: 2005, 2004, 2003

6 Bogle, Phantom, California

Family-owned, with 1,200 acres of vinyards in the Sacramento Delta, Bogle produces this blend of Petite Sirah with old-vine Syrah and Mourvèdre. Rich with plums, blackberries, spice, and sage, it is a dense, chewy style of wine.

Food pairings: Steak sandwich with salsa
Vintage years: 2005, 2004, 2002

7 Quady, Batch 88 Starboard, Madera

This is a non-vintage wine, blended from several vintages and aged for five years. This Tinta Roriz–dominated wine from vineyards in Madera and Amador acquires deep blackberry, prune, and chocolate flavors. Fortified to 20% alcohol, it cannot be called port, so it is called Starboard.

Food pairings: Chocolate desserts; full-flavored cheeses
Vintage years: NV

9 Ironstone Old Vine Reserve Zinfandel, Lodi

From vines over 45 years old at the large Ironstone property in the Sierra Foothills this Zin has dense, intense ripe cherry, licorice and cracked black pepper aromas with full-flavored blackberry fruit backed by grainy, minerally tannins.

Food pairings: Grilled ribs with a soy–ginger glaze
Vintage years: 2007, 2005, 2003

8 Terre Rouge, Syrah Ascent, Sierra Foothills

Based on the red volcanic-origin soils of Shenandoah Valley in Amador County, Terre Rouge specializes in Syrah. Coming from the best lots, Ascent is deeply concentrated with spiced blueberry fruit, smoky wood tones, and fine, silky tannins.

Food pairings: Duck breast with Port sauce
Vintage years: 2005, 2003, 2002

10 Boeger, Barbera, El Dorado

In the Sierra Foothills on steep slopes (around 2,000 feet), this old Gold Rush property makes a range of red wines including a juicy cherry, apple, and plum-infused Barbera, with spiced raspberry notes and a wonderful, lively finish.

Food pairings: Italian pork chops with mozzarella
Vintage years: 2007, 2006, 2005

An isolated vineyard in Central Valley, California

Oregon

Stretching from Portland to Eugene, the Willamette Valley has become home to America's best collection of Pinot Noirs. With wet winters and warm, dry summers, Pinot Noir ripens well to give some of the silky ethereal fruit this variety is famous for. Smaller subappellations, such as Dundee Hills and Eola-Amity Hills, are becoming known for their own characteristics.

A vineyard in Newberg, Oregon

1 Domaine Drouhin, Pinot Noir, Dundee Hills, Willamette Valley

Soft, pure Pinot Noir fruit comes from Véronique Drouhin, who makes the wines at this 90-acre hillside vineyard. High-density planting and meticulous winemaking produce elegant, textured wines with balance and length. Cuvée Laurène is the new top blend from selected barrels.

Food pairings: Duck breasts with parsnips and pears
Vintage years: 2006, 2004, 2002

2 William Hatcher, Pinot Noir, Willamette Valley

Bill Hatcher spent 14 years as winemaker and general manager at Domaine Drouhin. Now he selects grapes from four different sites to make the best wine for this label. Smooth, open-textured cherry fruit with refined tannins and a clean acidic balance.

Food pairings: Broiled fish such as salmon
Vintage years: 2005, 2004, 2003

4 Ponzi, Pinot Noir Reserve, Willamette Valley

A long-established family-run business with an excellent reputation. Using grapes from their own estates and surrounding growers, their wines have plum and white pepper aromas, lush cherry fruit, and a structured, lengthy finish.

Food pairings: Roast shoulder of lamb with fig and apricot stuffing
Vintage years: 2006, 2005, 2003

3 Firesteed, Pinot Noir, Willamette Valley

Without vineyards or a winery, this brand did more in the last decade to promote Oregon Pinot than many others. Consistently well made, it has black cherry fruit, with a touch of dark chocolate and smooth tannins. A new winery has now been acquired.

Food pairings: Slow-roasted lamb shanks with balsamic
Vintage years: 2007, 2006, 2005

5 King Estate, Domaine Pinot Noir, Oregon

Oregon's largest winery, with 465 acres of organic, dry-farmed vines. The Pinot has improved steadily as the vineyards have gained age and now shows supple, lithe fruit, with raspberry and cherry flavors and smooth, silky tannins.

Food pairings: Broiled fish or crab cakes
Vintage years: 2007, 2006, 2005

Washington State

Almost all of Washington's vineyards lie east of the Cascade Mountains, where long, hot, sunny summer days ripen Bordeaux varieties to perfection. Columbia Valley is used to describe many of the wines, to allow for some blending within the region, but specific areas such as Yakima, Horse Heaven Hills, and Red Mountain each have their own character. Farther east, Walla Walla is a fast-growing area, producing powerful, fruity red wines.

Washington State

Columbia Crest Winery, in Horse Heaven Hills

1 Chateau Ste. Michelle, Canoe Ridge Cabernet Sauvignon, Columbia Valley

The quality is good at this largest producer in Washington State. Canoe Ridge is a steep, south-facing slope on the banks of the Columbia River, producing ripe, concentrated, black cherry and blackberry fruit, wrapped in leather tones with elegant, dusty tannins.

Food pairings: Herb-stuffed lamb shoulder
Vintage years: 2004

2 Quilceda Creek, Cabernet Sauvignon, Columbia Valley

Now with a new winery, Quilceda Creek continues to make classy Cabernets from grapes grown on several prime sites. Blackberry, blueberry, and cassis fruit with nuances of dark chocolate and violets; good structure; and a complex, sleek finish.

Food pairings: Medium-rare sirloin steak
Vintage years: 2005, 2002, 2003

4 L'Ecole N°41, Pepper Bridge Vineyard Apogee, Walla Walla Valley

Based in an old schoolhouse, L'Ecole N°41 produces elegant wines from its own bought-in grapes. Apogee Red is a blend of Cabernet Sauvignon, Merlot, Malbec, and Cabernet Franc with bold, spicy, dark fruit, backed by sweet leather and coffee notes.

Food pairings: Beef or venison casseroles
Vintage years: 2006, 2005, 2003

3 Columbia Crest, Horse Heaven Hills Cabernet Sauvignon

Strong winds on the Horse Heaven Hills reduce canopy size and density, allowing better sun exposure on this south-facing, sandy slope. The result is blueberry, plum, and vanilla aromas and flavors with savory notes and a persistent finish.

Food pairings: Hamburgers with tomato-onion salsa
Vintage years: 2006, 2005, 2004

5 Cayuse Vineyards, Syrah, En Chamberlin Vineyard, Walla Walla

Names such as God Only Knows Grenache hide a serious intent. Low yields, rocky soils, and biodynamic cultivation produce deep, concentrated flavors. This Syrah has blackberry and plum fruit, sprinkled with white pepper, and a smooth generous finish.

Food pairings: Charcoal-grilled rib-eye steak
Vintage years: 2006, 2005, 2004

Southwest U.S. & Mexico

Thanks to the Spanish colonists of the sixteenth century, Mexico is home to some of America's oldest wineries. Now most of Mexico's vineyards are used to produce table grapes, raisins, and brandy, although there are significant wine-producing vineyards in select areas including the coastal area of Baja California and in Querétaro province, north of Mexico City. Texas had a head start in vine cultivation as the home of many indigenous vine species. It is now the fifth-largest wine-producing state, with the Texas High Plains in the northwest showing the best quality.

A Texan vineyard in the spring

1 L.A. Cetto, Petite Sirah, Valle de Guadalupe, Mexico

This is Mexico's biggest and most successful winery. It produces a range of wines, in particular Petite Sirah, Cabernets, Zinfandel, and Nebbiolo. This Petite Sirah has ripe, red-fruit flavors, with plummy notes and a juicy finish.

Food pairings: Roast chicken with salsa verde
Vintage years: 2007, 2006, 2004

2 Llano Estacado, Cabernet Sauvignon Cellar Reserve, Texas High Plains

Llano Estacado is now the largest premium winery in Texas, based in the Texas High Plains, 3,400 feet above sea level. This wine has soft, complex cherry and cassis fruit, with notes of cedar and well-balanced acidity.

Food pairings: Filet mignon with béarnaise sauce
Vintage years: 2006, 2005, 2004

3 Fall Creek, Meritus, Texas Hill Country, Austin, Texas

Made from a blend of Cabernet Sauvignon, Merlot, and Malbec grown on a former Texan cattle ranch, this is the premium wine, made only in exceptional years. Dense, full-bodied, and fruity, it gives a taste of the potential that is possible in Texas.

Food pairings: Texas rib-eye steak
Vintage years: 2004, 2003, 1999

4 Casa de Piedra, Vino do Sol, Guadalupe, Mexico

Based close to the coast in the Guadalupe Valley, with ocean breezes keeping temperatures down, Hugo d'Acosta makes a red wine from Tempranillo and Cabernet grapes. It has ripe, plummy fruit; soft tannins; and a smooth finish.

Food pairings: Steak fajitas
Vintage years: 2006, 2005, 2004

5 Casa Madero, Shiraz, Valle de Parras, Mexico

Founded in the late 1500s, this ancient winery in the fertile plains of the Parras Valley in central Mexico has brought in wine consultants from overseas to improve quality. The Shiraz has ripe, soft fruit with smoky, oaky tones.

Food pairings: Chicken enchiladas
Vintage years: 2006, 2004, 2001

1 ▮ 2 ▮▮ 3 ▮▮▮ 4 ▮ 5 ▮

New York State

Grape growing and winemaking in the eastern states of America are relatively new activities, but they are growing at a prodigious rate. New York State now has 250 wineries. This new expansion has seen many old *Vitis labrusca* vineyards—suitable for grape jelly, but less good for wine—replaced by wine-producing *Vitis vinifera*. Quality is improving all the time. The Finger Lakes region, just south of Lake Ontario, is the state's most important area for wine production, while the mild, temperate climate of Long Island provides a long growing season for Merlot and Cabernet.

Concord grapes are widely grown in upstate New York, and used especially to make kosher wine

① Millbrook, Cabernet Franc, Block Three East, Hudson River Region

Under the same ownership as Williams Selyem in Sonoma Coast, Millbrook's 30 acres are planted with Pinot Noir, Cabernet Franc, and some white varieties. Cabernet Franc shows good, juicy, red fruit, with lively cherry and tobacco notes and balanced, silky tannins.

Food pairings: Moroccan-spiced lamb or beef
Vintage years: 2006, 2005, 2000

② Fox Run, Pinot Noir Finger Lakes Reserve, Finger Lakes

Fox Run, on 55 acres overlooking Seneca Lake, is crafting a regional style, mainly for whites but also for Pinot Noir. This has light cherry fruit, with light oak and a refreshing style.

Food pairings: Pasta with summer vegetables and herbs
Vintage years: 2007, 2006, 2005

④ Bedell Cellars, Musée, North Fork, Long Island

A no-expense-spared high-quality operation with 78 acres of vines. The Musée is a Merlot-dominated blend, with Cabernet Sauvignon and Petit Verdot. It has plush cherry and cranberry fruit and a touch of spice backed by gentle tannins.

Food pairings: Lamb with rosemary
Vintage years: 2006, 2005

③ Lenz, Estate Selection Merlot, North Fork, Long Island

There are elegant and powerful reds at this 30-year-old winery with 70 acres of well-managed vineyards planted with *vinifera* varieties. This Estate Selection wine is aged in French oak and has rich, deep, velvety, red berry fruit with structured, ripe tannins.

Food pairings: Broiled chicken dishes
Vintage years: 2003, 2001

⑤ Wölffer, Estate Selection Merlot, The Hamptons, Long Island

There's a temperate, maritime climate at this stylish property just 3 miles from the Atlantic Ocean. This Merlot with 20 percent Cabernet Sauvignon has a complex aroma of figs, cedar, and prunes with a red-berried palate and fine tannins.

Food pairings: Aged hard cheese such as cheddar
Vintage years: 2004, 2003, 2001

Canada

The Canadian climate is generally not compatible with growing grapes; however, in regions where those wintery extremes are moderated by water, it is possible for vines to thrive. Canada is now establishing a reputation for quality as a whole and in particular for ice wine. In the east, Ontario is the established wine region, producing 80 percent of Canadian wine, mainly on the Niagara Peninsula next to Lake Ontario. Two thousand miles away, in British Columbia, conditions are similar to those in neighboring Washington State, and the warm, dry Okanagan Valley produces excellent reds.

A vineyard in Nova Scotia, Canada, where inexpensive land is facilitating a boom in wine production

1 Inniskillin, Cabernet Franc Icewine, Niagara Peninsula

From the original Inniskillin operation close to Lake Ontario, these grapes are harvested when frozen on the vine at temperatures of around 10°F. When crushed, they give tiny amounts of intense, sweet juice, which ferments into an exceptional strawberry-scented, vibrantly balanced sweet wine.

Food pairings: Perfect with raspberry pavlova
Vintage years: 2006, 2002

2 Jackson-Triggs, SunRock Vineyard Shiraz, Okanagan Valley

This company has feet firmly in both of Canada's major wine regions. This single-vineyard Shiraz from a mountain slope in the Okanagan Valley has a rich ruby color, with plum and pepper aromas, cloves, and smoky blueberries, with a long finish.

Food pairings: Mild Indian vegetable curries or ginger-spiced beef
Vintage years: 2006, 2005, 2004

4 Le Clos Jordanne, Village Reserve Pinot Noir, Niagara Peninsula

This Canadian–French partnership makes the most of the distinct Niagara terroir, with Chardonnay and Pinot Noir. This wine exhibits raspberry and mulberry aromas with smoky black fruits on the palate and a long, persistent finish.

Food pairings: Duck with maple syrup glaze
Vintage years: 2006, 2004

3 Mission Hill, Merlot S.L.C., Okanagan Valley

Overlooking Lake Okanagan, Mission Hill has been at the forefront of British Columbia's wine industry for decades. Five vineyards within the Okanagan Valley provide grapes for the Select Lot Collection (S.L.C.). This Merlot provides bright cherry fruit, herbs, and a rich texture.

Food pairings: Roasted fig-and-plum-stuffed pork
Vintage years: 2005, 2004, 2003

5 Inniskillin Dark Horse Vineyard, Meritage, Okanagan Valley

The British Columbian outpost of this Ontario-founded company is now making a fine range of wines. This Merlot-dominated Meritage blend is deep-colored, with ripe, chocolate-dipped cherry notes and firm, ripe tannins.

Food pairings: Pot-roasted venison
Vintage years: 2006, 2005

CHILE

ARGENTINA URUGUAY

- Brasília

- Salta

La Serena ●
Santiago ●
Mendoza ●
Neuquén ●
Concepción ●
Buenos Aires ●

South America

After Europe, South America is the world's most important wine-producing continent. Vines arrived with the Spanish in the early sixteenth century and were planted first in Mexico and then in Peru, Chile, and Argentina. Over the centuries, successive waves of immigration from Europe—particularly from Portugal, Italy, and France—have influenced the wine culture throughout South America. Now Argentina is South America's most important wine producer by far, in terms of quantity, although exports have helped Chile establish a respected international profile ahead of its neighbor.

These twin powerhouses of South American wine production are poised on either side of the majestic Andes Mountains, less than 100 miles apart, yet separated by a 20,000-foot-high jagged ridge of rock and ice. In Argentina the mighty Malbec is king, producing wines with deep, blackberry-soaked fruit. Chile is famous for its lush, fruity Cabernet Sauvignons, but delicate Pinot Noirs are finding a home here too.

Brazil is the continent's third most important producer, and it makes considerable amounts of sparkling wine; however, with a local population of 180 million, there has not been any need to export seriously. Uruguay is learning to tame its famous Tannat grape and is now starting to work on its export markets, while Peru is a major producer of grapes for the local spirit, Pisco.

Argentina

Argentina is the fifth largest wine producing country in the world and is rapidly moving forward in quality. Its vineyards are concentrated in the west of the country, in the shelter of the Andes Mountains where rainfall is naturally low but snow on top of the mountains provides more than enough water for irrigation.

Altitude is the key to Argentina's wine regions. As the land rises to meet the Andes, vineyards at altitudes that range from 2,000 feet to 5,000 feet provide varying daytime and nighttime temperatures to ripen a whole selection of grapes, from light aromatic whites to deep-flavored reds.

 Salta

❶ Salta
❷ Mendoza & Uco Valley
❸ Patagonia

ARGENTINA

Argentina is subject to a variety of climates. As a rule, the climate is predominantly temperate with extremes ranging from subtropical in the north to subpolar in the far south. Central Argentina has hot summers with thunderstorms, and cold winters.

Mendoza & Uco Valley

The wine-growing region of Mendoza, centered on the city of the same name, accounts for around 70 percent of Argentina's wine production. Malbec is the most important red grape variety here, and the vineyards of Central Mendoza, around Luján de Cuyo, are particularly famed for their quality. Farther south, at altitudes that reach 5,000 feet, is Argentina's most exciting new region, the Uco Valley, where warm days and chilly nights keep freshness and flavor in the grapes.

Mendoza

Mendoza

7
8
9
4
3
10
2

6
Uco Valley
1
5

A worker picks Malbec grapes at the Familia Zuccardi vineyard in Maipu

1 Clos de los Siete, Mendoza

A joint venture wine from six investors in the cool Uco Valley with wine guru Michel Rolland in charge. Malbec-based, with Merlot, Cabernet Sauvignon, and Syrah in the blend, this excellent, affordable wine has bold, ripe, black-fruit flavors with savory licorice notes and increasing finesse.

Food pairings: Braised oxtail in red wine
Vintage years: 2007, 2006, 2005

2 Zuccardi Q, Malbec, Mendoza

Innovation is key at this large, dynamic company in North Mendoza where the emphasis is on organic or near-organic cultivation. This Malbec is loaded with fine cherry and violet-scented fruit with tobacco-leaf and licorice notes on the palate leading to a powerful, long finish.

Food pairings: Mushroom-stuffed beef tenderloin
Vintage years: 2007, 2006, 2002

4 Kaiken, Ultra Malbec, Mendoza

Winemaker Aurelio Montes from Chile manages to produce a wine that is initially restrained on the nose, then opens on the palate with powerful bramble fruit, cherries, and tobacco leading to smooth tannins and serious complexity.

Food pairings: Plain broiled steak or cheesy zucchini casseroles
Vintage years: 2006, 2005, 2004

3 Catena Alta, Malbec, Mendoza

This large company hits the right notes at all price levels. High-altitude vineyards produce aromas of dark-berry fruits, cloves, and cedar with rich cassis flavors, hints of chocolate, and black pepper. Ripe, fine-grained tannins mean this wine ages well

Food pairings: All red meats or steak and kidney pie
Vintage years: 2006, 2005, 2004.

5 O. Fournier, Alfa Crux Malbec, Mendoza

Old vines, cool climate, and meticulous selection at this top-notch estate produce wines with sweet, fat, plum and cherry fruit; layers of chocolate and tobacco; and structuring tannins on the finish. Enjoyable now, this wine will expand and improve over the next five years.

Food pairings: Cumin-spiced lamb curry
Vintage years: 2006, 2005, 2002

6 Finca Sophenia, Synthesis The Blend, Tupungato, Mendoza

Finca Sophenia's top wine selected from each year's best barrels of Malbec, Cabernet Sauvignon, and Merlot. Has the delicate scent of violets, mixed with fresh-berried dark fruits, a spicy expression of fruit on the palate, and a complex, chewy finish. Ages well.

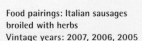

Food pairings: Italian sausages broiled with herbs
Vintage years: 2007, 2006, 2005

7 Fabre Montmayou, Gran Reserva Malbec, Vistalba, Mendoza

Century-old Malbec vines, densely planted and deeply rooted in Vistalba, produce lush, ripe, bramble fruit that is cosseted into French-accented, silky, spicy style by French owner and winemaker Hervé Joyaux.

Food pairings: Simple broiled steak with fried potatoes
Vintage years: 2007, 2006, 2005

9 Pascual Toso, Syrah, Mendoza

Long established producer in warm, eastern part of Mendoza making refreshingly modern-style wines. This Syrah is a bold, blackberry-drenched wine with a touch of raspberry juiciness. Good, balanced oak and chocolaty tannins round off the finish. Great value.

Food pairings: Chorizo and lentil stew
Vintage years: 2007, 2006, 2005

8 Cheval des Andes, Vistalba, Mendoza

This joint venture blends expertise of Château Cheval Blanc of St Emilion and dense fruit flavors from old Argentine vines. Malbec-based, with Cabernet Sauvignon, Merlot, and Petit Verdot in the blend; vibrant with chocolate-dipped raspberry, dusted with spice, and finished with silky tannins.

Food pairings: Crown roast of lamb
Vintage years: 2005, 2004, 2002

10 Achaval Ferrer Quimera, Mendoza

Distinctive wine from meticulous producer. A splash of Cabernet Franc in a blend of Malbec, Merlot, and Cabernet Sauvignon adds clean, fresh notes, allowing dark mulberry fruit to shine. The palate is laced with licorice notes and ends in a pleasant, ripe, tannic structure.

Food pairings: Oven-roasted lamb with anise and rosemary
Vintage years: 2007, 2006, 2005

A vineyard in the Tupungato region, Mendoza

Salta

This stunningly beautiful wine-growing region, 600 miles north of Mendoza, is located at 24–26 degrees of latitude, so it should be too warm to grow quality grapes, but its situation in the foothills of the Andes means that it has some of the highest vineyards in the world. Most of the region is at 5,000 feet above sea-level, and new plantations climb even higher to 7,500 feet and beyond. The main wine producing area is in the Calchaquí Valley, where Malbec, Cabernet Sauvignon, and Tannat all do well. Old vines and low yields produce remarkably densely flavored wines.

ARGENTINA

Salta

4

Salta

3 1 2 5

The combination of warm days with bright sunshine and cool nights keeps flavors fresh in Salta

1 Quara, Reserve Tannat, Cafayate

With fine, ripe tannins, elegant blackberry fruit, and touches of chocolate-dipped prunes, this wine shows just how good Tannat can be. It comes from the historic, white-painted bodega of Lavaque in the Cafayate Valley, 5,000 feet above sea level.

Food pairings: Hamburgers or vegetarian dishes such as mushroom and eggplant casserole
Vintage years: 2006, 2005, 2004

2 Michel Torino, Don David Tannat, Cafayate

This historic 2,000-acre estate has a white-painted colonial-style bodega, now a luxury hotel, at its heart. Old, organically grown Tannat vines grown in the rocky soil produce a concentrated wine with complex aromas of cloves and dark fruits followed by dark chocolate and prune flavors.

Food pairings: Calves' liver with onions
Vintage years: 2006, 2005, 2004

4 Bodega Colomé, Estate Malbec, Calchaquí Valley

From one of the highest vineyards in the world, and made from mainly Malbec with a splash of Cabernet Sauvignon and Tannat, this is an iconic wine, intense with masses of black fruit; sweet, spicy notes; and black pepper.

Food pairings: Beef casserole with thyme
Vintage years: 2006, 2005, 2004

3 San Pedro de Yacochuya, Malbec, Cafayate

This is In one of world's most remote vineyard locations. Mainly Malbec with splash of Cabernet Sauvignon. Intense and savory with layers of strawberry and blackberry fruit and notes of licorice and spice in a harmonious tannic frame.

Food pairings: Standing rib roast
Vintage years: 2004, 2003, 2000

5 Etchart Arnaldo B Gran Reserva, Cafayate

Established in 1850, Etchart owns 750 acres of vines in the high altitude Salta region. This is Malbec-dominated with Cabernet Sauvignon, oak-aged for 18 months and has dense bramble fruit, with figs, coffee, and mineral notes followed by rounded, supple tannins.

Food pairings: Beef and olive empañadas
Vintage years: 2006, 2005, 2004

   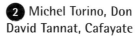 

Patagonia

Five hundred miles south of Mendoza, in northern Patagonia, is the Rio Negro region where flat desert stretches to infinity. Two centuries ago, part of the desert became an oasis of agriculture after channels were dug to divert meltwater from the Andes into a steep-sided valley. Increasing numbers of vineyards benefit from the cool climate. Ripening times are long and slow here, and wines reflect that with increased finesse. Among others, Pinot Noir is showing great potential and even Syrah ripen fully to produce outstanding wines. Another 400 miles south, in the region of Chubut, more vineyards are being planted.

Malbec grapes on the vine, Patagonia

➊ Familia Schroeder, Saurus Patagonia Select Malbec

Old Malbec vines on this 275-acre property in the valley of San Patricio del Chañar provide deep, expressive, mulberry fruit flavors with shades of leather, coffee, and violets. Ripe, silky tannins give way to a long, balanced, vanilla-licked finish.

Food pairings: Grilled hamburgers and kabobs
Vintage years: 2006, 2005, 2004

➋ Bodega Noemia, J. Alberto Malbec, Río Negro

Next door to Chacra and using Malbec grapes from those same historic vineyards, this wine is made from 95 percent Malbec and just 5 percent Merlot. Dark with black, dense fruit, layered with chocolate and spice, and balanced by coffee tones, this is opulent and powerful.

Food pairings: Seared venison medallions
Vintage years: 2007, 2006, 2005

➍ Chacra, Treinta y Dos, Pinot Noir, Patagonia

Vines planted in 1932, now farmed biodynamically by Piero Incisa della Rocchetta (whose family also owns Italian icon Sassicaia), produce tiny quantities of top-quality Pinot Noir. With blackberry and black cherry concentration; a silky palate; and complex minerality on the finish.

Food pairings: Roast duck with juniper berries
Vintage years: 2007, 2006, 2004

➌ Domaine Vistalba, Viñalba Patagonia Malbec Syrah

A deep purple color with concentrated blackberry fruit on the nose. On the palate are ripe, dense, black fruits with floral, savory notes, a firm structure, and a long savory finish.

Food pairings: Braised chicken with cilantro
Vintage years: 2007, 2006

➎ Humberto Canale Black River Malbec, Río Negro

Based in the Upper Valley, this family business combines old vineyards and new technology to produce intense, deep-flavored wines. Rich with black cherry fruit, damsons, and figs, blending with bitter chocolate on the palate and balanced acidity on a seamless finish.

Food pairings: Mature cheese
Vintage years: 2008, 2007, 2006

Chile

In a country that spans 3,000 miles from north to south, with an inexhaustible supply of irrigation water and clear, reliable sunshine, it is inevitable that there would be many suitable sites for vineyards. The Central Valley, tucked between the Andes and the coastal range, is the powerhouse of Chile's wine production, with the ripe, richly scented fruit of Cabernet Sauvignon as its most favored grape.

Now, as water boreholes and pipelines permit, new areas are opening up to viticulture, providing more challenging sites for different grape varieties. Cooler, coastal areas such as Elqui, Limarí, and San Antonio are being developed with Pinot Noir and Syrah as the real success stories among the reds. Carmenère has also been rediscovered after being wrongly labeled as Merlot for generations. Its deep, fruity, spice-edged flavors are a signature of Chile's most distinctive wines.

1 Limari & Elqui
2 Aconcagua Valley
3 Central Valley

CHILE

The Chilean climate ranges
from arid in the north to
glacial in the southeast.
The wine producing area
benefits from the proximity
of the Andes, which create a
steep drop in temperatures
overnight, maintaining the
grapes' acidity levels.

Santiago

CHILE

Aconcagua Valley

The Aconcagua Valley is a warm, dry region, where temperatures are somewhat moderated by the twin effects of cool air from the Andes in the east and Pacific breezes in the west. This is very much a red wine region with Cabernet Sauvignon and Syrah doing well. Farther south, and within easy reach of the Pacific, the subregion of Casablanca Valley draws morning fog into the valley. Discovered suitable for vines in the 1980s, new plantings of Pinot Noir show great finesse and elegance. The new and exciting subregion of San Antonio is even closer to the coast yet its rolling hills provide good growing conditions.

Erecting wooden stakes in vineyard, Aconcaqua Valley, Chile

❶ Casa Marin Miramar Vineyard, Syrah, San Antonio

Just 3 miles from the coast and with a sometimes foggy seaview, the blustery vineyards of this small boutique winery are on calcareous clay soil, which produces a blueberry-soaked, peppery-spiced, tight-structured Syrah. This is one of Chile's most exciting new wineries.

Food pairings: Grilled chicken or coq au vin
Vintage years: 2005, 2004, 2003

❷ Matetic, Syrah EQ, San Antonio

A small, family-run company producing very impressive wines using biodynamic methods. This is one of Chile's best Syrahs, with intense blackberry fruit laced with spice; a dense, earthy palate; and a long, chocolate-tinged finish.

Food pairings: Charcoal-grilled red meat
Vintage years: 2006, 2005, 2003

❹ Viña Leyda Cahuil, Pinot Noir, San Antonio

Just 10 miles from the Pacific, Leyda Valley is buffeted by a cool summer breeze that keeps temperatures down and blows pests away. The result is this crunchy, juicy, strawberry-stashed Pinot Noir, which still has enough depth and complexity to accompany broiled lamb.

Food pairings: Broiled lamb
Vintage years: 2007, 2006, 2005

❸ Amayna, Pinot Noir, San Antonio

Low yields, a cool climate, and a new gravity-fed winery are key factors in this fresh-tasting Pinot Noir. With wild raspberry aromas, dark cherry fruit on the palate, and subtle oak on the finish, it is bigger in flavor than most Chilean Pinots.

Food pairings: Broiled salmon with lentils
Vintage years: 2006, 2005, 2004

❺ Seña, Aconcagua Valley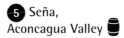

A rocky, densely planted, biodynamically run vineyard in the western part of the Aconcagua Valley, where afternoon breezes keep temperatures down. Still young, this iconic wine is dense with layers of black-berried fruit, coffee, spice, and tobacco.

Food pairings: Roast wild duck, or seared beef fillet
Vintage years: 2005, 2003, 2001

❶ 　❷ 　❸ 　❹ 　❺

6 Errazuriz Don Maximiano Founder's Reserve, Aconcagua Valley

High-density, low-yielding vines in the warm Panquehue subregion of Aconcagua produce this luxurious, powerful Cabernet-dominated blend with complex blackcurrant, fig, and coffee notes, a rounded smooth palate, and creamy, silky tannins.

Food pairings: Anise and garlic spiced daube of beef
Vintage years: 2005, 2004, 2003

7 Viña Cono Sur, 20 Barrels Pinot Noir, Casablanca Valley

Part of the Concha y Toro empire, but operated separately, Cono Sur makes exceptional Pinot Noirs at all price levels. This top-notch version combines dark, elegant cherry and raspberry fruit with depth of flavor and sophisticated complexity on the finish.

Food pairings: Wild mushroom risotto
Vintage years: 2007, 2006, 2005

9 Loma Larga, Cabernet Franc, Casablanca Valley

Grown on a hillside location in the cool, sea-breezy part of Casablanca Valley, this fresh-tasting wine is full of raspberry-edged, juicy, crunchy berries, with notes of sage and thyme cutting across the palate, leading to a long, fruit-soaked finish.

Food pairings: Zucchini and red bell pepper casserole
Vintage years: 2007, 2006, 2005

8 Kingston Family Vineyards, Tobiano Pinot Noir, Casablanca Valley

This cattle ranch planted 200 acres of vines in the coolest southwest part of Casablanca. Results are excellent and this Pinot shows deep, dark-raspberry fruit; a touch of herbs; and a sprinkle of black pepper with a balanced, elegant finish.

Food pairings: Fettucine with sun-dried tomatoes
Vintage years: 2007, 2006, 2005

10 Veramonte, Cabernet Sauvignon Primus, Casablanca Valley

Most of the Veramonte estate is a nature reserve, but the 1,000-acre vineyard produces deep-flavored, concentrated wines. Primus is the top wine, a rich, blackberry-infused blend of Merlot, Cabernet Sauvignon, and Carmenère.

Food pairings: Peppercorn-dusted steak
Vintage years: 20056, 2005, 2001

Must samples and grapes, Don Maximiano Vineyard

Central Valley

Occupying the land between the Andean foothills and the coastal range of hills, the Central Valley runs for 200 miles south from Santiago. Cutting across it are subvalleys formed by rivers; these form Chile's great wine-producing regions of Maipo, Cachapoal, Colchagua, Curicó, and Maule, each with its own particular climate and growing conditions. Cabernet Sauvignon is the most widely planted grape variety, although Merlot, Carmenère, and some white varieties do well, depending on the vineyard altitude and its proximity to the cooling effect of the Andes.

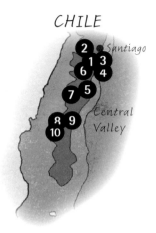

CHILE

Santiago

Central Valley

The 1996 vintage of the Almaviva Puente Alto

1 Alvaro Espinoza, Antiyal, Maipo

Deep intense flavors from Chile's leading organic and bio dynamic winemaker. Made from a blend of Carmenère, Cabernet Sauvignon, and Syrah, it is packed with black cherry and blackberry fruit, with tobacco, a touch of spice, and a firm, structured finish.

Food pairings: Roasted red meats; cheese-topped roasted root vegetables
Vintage years: 2005, 2004, 2003

2 Santa Rita Medalla Real Cabernet Sauvignon

Great value from one of Chile's oldest wineries and their 5,000 acres of vineyards. Cabernet with a splash of Merlot, this wine is broad-shouldered with deep color and flavor, ripe black currant and cedar notes, savory tobacco flavors, and fine-grained tannins.

Food pairings: Lamb crown roast, prime rib
Vintage years: 2006, 2005, 2004

4 Concha y Toro, Terrunyo Cabernet Sauvignon, Maipo

From a selected block within the well-drained, stony Las Terrazas vineyard in Pirque, this wine spends 17 months in French oak. It is full of expressive black cherry and cassis fruit with pencil shavings, spice, and an oak-tinged, clean finish.

Food pairings: Broiled lamb chops
Vintage years: 2006, 2005, 2004

3 Almaviva Puente Alto, Maipo

A joint-venture wine between Concha y Toro and Baron Philippe de Rothschild based in Tocornal vineyard in Puente Alto. Bordeaux-blend, aged 18 months in French oak, with powerful black currant and blackberry fruit; earthy, mineral notes; and mocha, chocolate, and licorice.

Food pairings: Crown roast of lamb
Vintage years: 2005, 2004, 2001

5 Viña La Rosa, Don Reca Merlot Cabernet Sauvignon, Cachapoal

From one of the most beautiful wine estates in Chile, tucked away in a hidden valley and surrounded by palm trees, comes this warm-fruited, complex wine, full of velvety red currant and plum flavors, silky tannins, and a long, lingering, oak-edged finish.

Food pairings: Slow-cooked lamb shanks
Vintage years: 2006, 2005, 2004

6 Cousiño-Macul, Finis Terrae, Maipo

A new estate and winery in Buin have replaced old vineyards, and now Cousiño-Macul wines have fresher, more elegant flavors. Finis Terrae is a Cabernet Sauvignon–Merlot blend with ripe plum and mocha notes, hints of sage, and a vanilla-edged, firm, finish.

Food pairings: Lamb casserole with olives
Vintage years: 2006, 2005, 2003

7 Casa Lapostolle, Cuvée Alexandre Merlot, Colchagua

Old vines, attention to detail, and skilled winemaking are the key quality factors at this property in Colchagua. Opulent, ripe red and black currants dominate this wine, with hints of rosemary, white pepper, and basil, and a creamy long finish.

Food pairings: Venison medallions
Vintage years: 2006, 2005, 2004

9 Viñedos Orgánicos Emiliana, Coyam, Colchagua

One of Chile's most remarkable wines. Alvaro Espinoza heads this totally integrated biodynamic farm at Los Robles, owned by the Guilisasti family. Syrah, Merlot, Carmenère, Cabernet Sauvignon, and Malbec grapes give a rich, savory style, dense with fruit, herbs, and spice.

Food pairings: Finest beef fillet
Vintage years: 2006, 2005, 2004

8 Montes Alpha, Syrah, Colchagua

Aurelio Montes was the first to plant Syrah on the higher slopes of Apalta in Colchagua Valley. The benefits of that breezy site are obvious in this wine, with its dense, dark, smoky bramble fruit; coffee; ripe, supple tannins; and long expressive finish.

Food pairings: Grilled red meats
Vintage years: 2006, 2005, 2004

10 Casa Silva, Doña Dominga Reserva Carmenère, Colchagua

A long-established company, now with a vibrant new lease of life. Carmenère is the real strength, and this great value version provides dark brambly fruit, intensely spicy flavors, and a rounded, clean finish.

Food pairings: Paprika-rubbed pork roast
Vintage years: 2007, 2006, 2005

6 ❙❙   7 ❙❙   8 ❙❙   9 ❙❙❙❙❙   10 ❙

A wine-grower riding through a vineyard, Santa Rita

Limarí & Elqui

The arid northern vineyards of Limarí and Elqui, 250 miles north of Santiago, were once used only for growing grapes for the local spirit, Pisco. Now, plantings of wine grapes are increasing as these regions are explored for their suitability for Cabernet Sauvignon, Merlot, Syrah, and Carmenère. Temperatures in these northern regions are moderated by the cooling effect of breezes from the Pacific Ocean, while in Elqui a morning fog blankets the region, keeping temperatures down. New vineyard sites up to 6,500 feet are being planted.

A vineyard in Limarí, where cooling breezes moderate the hot temperatures

1 Tabalí, Reserva Syrah, Limarí

Long sun-soaked days and cold nights develop complexity in the grapes for this deep-colored, serious wine. With wild cherries, dusted with white pepper notes, hints of smoke, and an elegant, supple tannin structure, this is a fresh style of wine from a great new region.

Food pairings: Chile-spiced beef or vegetable casserole
Vintage years: 2007, 2006, 2004

2 Viña Casa Tamaya, Carmenère Reserve, Limarí

Close to the Pacific and cooled by afternoon breezes, 500 acres of new vineyard produce grapes at this state-of-the-art winery. This Carmenère has deep blackberry and cassis aromas, overtones of black pepper and chocolate on the palate, and a supple structure.

Food pairings: Pasta or roasted root vegetables with cheese
Vintage years: 2007, 2006, 2005

4 Viña Mayu, Carmenère Reserva, Elqui

Viña Mayu is a new off-shoot of Viña Falernia, making quality wines from their high-altitude vineyard carved out of the desert. This Carmenère has bright bramble fruit, notes of spice, roasted game, and cracked black pepper with ripe, supple tannins.

Food pairings: Beef casserole with olives
Vintage years: 2007, 2006

3 Maycas Del Limarí, Reserva Especial Syrah, Limarí Valley

With 1000 acres of newly planted vines across the Limarí Valley, this winery is already turning out stunning wines. Clear skies and high-intensity sunshine have produced an intense wine, full of chewy, savory blackberry fruit with a rich chocolaty finish. Great value.

Food pairings: Pheasant or pork casserole
Vintage years: 2007, 2006, 2005

5 Maycas Del Limarí, Reserva Especial Cabernet Sauvignon, Limarí Valley

Dense, chewy elegant Cabernets from this cool, maritime climate. High luminosity promotes thicker grape skins and so the wines acquire a dense color, rich in cassis and blackberry fruit, with supple tannins and a structured finish.

Food pairings: Rosemary-studded lamb
Vintage years: 2007, 2006, 2005

Uruguay & Brazil

Grape growing in Uruguay is concentrated on the clay soils of the coastal Canalones region around Montevideo. Here, the major red grape variety—Tannat—ripens well in the relatively cool climate, producing sturdy blackberry fruit flavors and fine-structured tannins. In recent years there has been new investment in vineyards and wineries. Following international investment, Brazil's wine industry is at last moving forward. Most vineyards are concentrated in the high, hilly Serra Gaúcha in the south of the country, but the new, drier region of Fronteira on less fertile soils is showing promise.

Petit Verdot is often used as a blending grape, but can produce excellent wines too, like the Pisano

① Bouza, Tannat, Canalones, Uruguay

This smart, modern winery has learned how to tame its Tannat by individual grape selection, gentle maceration, and long aging in French and American oak. The wine has an intense garnet color, with aromas of dark plummy, figgy fruit and a supple, tannic structure.

② Juanicó, Don Pascual Tannat Roble, Canalones, Uruguay

Chalky soils on the gentle rolling hills in the southern part of the Canalones region produce this intensely deep-colored wine, with inky, spicy fruit and chocolate and coffee notes on the long, structured finish.

Food pairings: Lamb tagine
Vintage years: 2007, 2006, 2005

③ Pizzorno, Merlot Tannat, Canalones, Uruguay

From a family-run company in the heart of Canalones, this is a softer style of Tannat, mellowed by a substantial proportion of Merlot, giving a rounded, structured, savory, meaty wine with ripe, blackberry fruit and a long finish.

Food pairings: Slow-cooked lamb shanks
Vintage years: 2006, 2005, 2004

④ Pisano RPF Family Personal Reserve Petit Verdot, Uruguay

Tiny quantities of Petit Verdot from a small plot at this family-owned winery in the Progresso area just north of Montevideo. Small berries and thick grape skins give the wine a deep, red-purple color with the aroma of spicy black pepper and ripe red fruits.

Food pairings: Grilled spareribs
Vintage years: 2006, 2005, 2004

⑤ Miolo, Merlot Terroir, Brazil

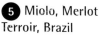

This company recruited international wine consultant Michel Rolland, and the results are starting to show in the wines. This is a ruby-colored wine with an intense blueberry nose and a good, deep structure.

Food pairings: After dinner with robust mature cheese
Vintage years: 2005, 2004

Food pairings: Broiled beef rump with rosemary
Vintage years: 20047, 2006, 2005

AUSTRALIA

Western
Australia

South
Australia

New
South
Wales

Victoria

Tasmania

Perth

Adelaide

Sydney

Melbourne

Hobart

Australia

Vine cuttings arrived in Australia via the Cape in the late eighteenth century and so began an industry which has spread across Australia and is now the sixth largest in the world. Initially the bulk of production was fortified wines and it has been only in the last few decades that the focus has shifted to table wines.

Grapes are grown in every state and territory of Australia, taking advantage of the wide range of climates and conditions across this vast land, but the main focus is in the southeastern corner, with South Australia leading the way. This state accounts for over 40 percent of the vineyards and over 50 percent of the output. It is a powerhouse of production, ranging from the irrigated Riverlands producing vast amounts of easy-drinking wine, to the specialist areas such as the cool-climate Adelaide Hills, the warm Barossa, and the red-soil of Coonawarra.

Victoria is the smallest of the mainland states, yet it is second in terms of wine production. Its cool coastal climate regions produce delicate Pinots, while the dry heat of Rutherglen is just perfect for fortified red wines.

With its vineyards just a few hours' drive from Sydney, the Hunter Valley has become a destination as well as an important wine region. New cooler areas of this state are opening up, with the altitude of Orange providing cooler climates for more expressive wines.

Over in Western Australia, coastal breezes and fashionable lifestyle producers create an added dimension for this continent's diverse and delicious wines.

South Australia

With Adelaide acting as hub, the vineyards of South Australia spread out, north and south, taking advantage of different climates, soils, and altitudes. The Barossa Valley is the best-known region, famous for its deep-flavored Shiraz, which thrives on the warm valley floor. Farther north, Clare Valley's most distinctive wine, Riesling, occupies the cool hills, but in the warmer folds of the hills, Cabernet Sauvignon and Shiraz acquire vibrancy and character. The lush Adelaide Hills produce some of Australia's best Pinot Noir, while McLaren Vale is home to a group of dynamic, individual producers who harness the maritime climate to create distinctive vibrant wines.

While Coonawarra has had years to establish its reputation for Cabernet Sauvignon, nearby Wrattonbully, Padthaway, and Mount Benson are only recently developing their own styles. Finally there is the heartbeat of the region, the hot, flat, irrigated land alongside the Murray River in the north. This Riverland is responsible for a huge volume of wine, yet in the light of recent droughts it may have an uncertain future.

1 Clare Valley
2 Barossa
3 Adelaide Hills
4 Fleurieu
5 Limestone Coast

SOUTH AUSTRALIA

Covering some of the most
arid parts of the Australian
landmass, South Australia
also experiences cooler
temperatures in the Adelaide
Hills and the Limestone Coast.

Barossa

This is one of Australia's most famous wine regions, first settled by Silesian immigrants and now home to many of Australia's famous companies such as Penfolds, Jacob's Creek, and Yalumba. It has a warm climate and a tradition of producing powerful Shiraz-based wines. Other Rhône grapes such as Grenache and Mourvèdre also do well, and there are some stunning Cabernets too. Close by is the cooler, more elevated Eden Valley, which excels at white wines, but also produces some elegant red varieties, particularly Cabernets.

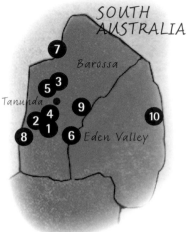

Picking grapes by hand, Peter Lehmanns, Barossa Valley

1. Grant Burge, Filsell Old Vine Shiraz, Barossa Valley

Ninety-year-old Shiraz vines provide the fruit for this wine, and the concentration in the grapes shows. This is a powerful wine, with chocolate-dipped blackberry aromas, complex fleshy fruit on the palate, subtle oak, and velvety tannins with a lift of acidity on the finish.

Food pairings: Beef Bourguignonne
Vintage years: 2005, 2004, 2003

2. John Duval, Entity, Barossa Valley

After years at Penfolds, responsible for Grange, Australia's icon wine, John Duval now makes his own handcrafted wines. This intense, fine-structured Shiraz has blackberry, blueberry and coffee notes; a full-bodied, balanced palate, depth, juicy acidity, and a long, pure-fruited finish.

Food pairings: Hard cheeses like cheddar and Parmesan
Vintage years: 2006, 2005, 2004

4. Glaetzer, Bishop Shiraz, Barossa Valley

There has been increasing focus and expression at Glaetzer in recent years. Top wines Amon-Ra and Anaperenna are outstanding and expensive. Bishop is more affordable and available, yet still has classic cherry and black pepper fruit, a touch of licorice, supple tannins, and an ability to age.

Food pairings: Corn and green chile casserole
Vintage years: 2006, 2005, 2004

3. Peter Lehmann, Eight Songs Shiraz, Barossa Valley

Old Barossa Shiraz vines produce concentrated fruit for this smooth and character-full wine. Fermented in new, 100 percent French oak hogsheads, the wine is smooth, round, and generous with dark plum and mocha-chocolate notes with vanilla undertones and velvety tannins.

Food pairings: Braised beef in red wine
Vintage years: 2004, 2002, 2000

5. Langmeil, Valley Floor Shiraz, Barossa Valley

Dry-farmed old Shiraz vines, open fermenters, and basket presses are just some of the quality factors at this business. Valley Floor Shiraz is full of dark blueberry, plum, and currant fruit; laced with spiced oak; and ending with a rich, ripe, sweet finish.

Food pairings: Mushroom and eggplant moussaka
Vintage years: 2006, 2005, 2004

6 Charles Melton, Nine Popes, Barossa Valley

One of the first Barossa wines to blend Shiraz, Grenache, and Mourvèdre together, Nine Popes is still on form and bursting with flavor. Black cherry and tobacco notes with meaty, savory tones and a plummy, spicy finish.

Food pairings: Rib-eye steak
Vintage years: 2005, 2003, 2001

7 Barossa Valley Estates E Minor Shiraz, Barossa Valley

Established as a growers' cooperative and now owned by one of the giants of Australian winemaking. Quality is still high and this wine, at the affordable end of the range, is bright, lively with juicy blackberry and raspberry fruit and a savory finish.

Food pairings: Steak sandwich
Vintage years: 2006, 2005, 2004

9 Yalumba, Hand-Picked Mourvèdre Grenache Shiraz, Barossa Valley

Australia's oldest family-owned winery makes this fine blend of Southern French varietals. It is deep-colored, with blackberry and prune aromas, sweet black fruits and coffee on the palate, and ripe, plush tannins.

Food pairings: Chicken stew with beans
Vintage years: 2006, 2005, 2004

8 Schild Estate, Shiraz, Barossa Valley

This family-run estate takes grapes from seven sites across the Barossa with the aim of reflecting the Barossa terroir. It is full of smooth, ripe cherry and blackberry fruit, overlaid with sweet spice, and a touch of mocha on the finish.

Food pairings: Hamburgers with tomato salsa
Vintage years: 2006, 2005, 2004

10 Henschke, Johann's Garden, Eden Valley

Fabulous reds come from this exceptional producer, most of them at exceptional prices. This is a new addition—a Grenache-dominated blend with a sweet, ripe, and spice-dusted raspberry nose; a lush, rich palate with velvety tannins; and a long, balanced finish.

Food pairings: Cumin-spiced lamb curry
Vintage years: 2006, 2005, 2004

6 ||| 7 | 8 || 9 ||| 10 |||

Old wine press at Yalumba Winery, Barossa Valley

Clare Valley

Clare is the northernmost vineyard area in South Australia. This region relies on its altitude and cool breezes to keep temperatures down. Structure, elegance, and complexity are the key descriptors for wines from this region, especially among the succulent, firm Cabernets and gentle, spicy Shiraz.

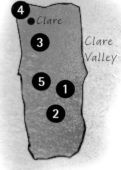

SOUTH AUSTRALIA

Clare

Clare Valley

Landscape of vines in Clare Valley

1 Grosset, Gaia, Clare Valley

Grapes for this wine come from a stony, windswept vineyard at 1,700 feet, high above the cornfields of the Clare Valley. The wine is a Cabernet Sauvignon–dominated Meritage blend and manages deep, brambly, black currant fruit, with succulence, weight, and density.

Food pairings: Herb-crusted rack of lamb
Vintage years: 2005, 2004, 2002

2 Wakefield, Estates Shiraz, Clare Valley

Clare Valley's biggest producer, with overall good quality. St Andrew's Shiraz is one of the top wines, with sweet plum fruit and firm tannins, but this Estates Shiraz offers delicious blackberry and cherry fruit with layers of tobacco and a tight structure with refined tannins.

Food pairings: Anything off the grill
Vintage years: 2007, 2006, 2004

4 Jim Barry, McRae Wood Shiraz, Clare Valley

A deep-colored, full-bodied, juicy Shiraz, with ripe raspberry and black currant fruit; a rich, concentrated palate with plums, licorice, and a faint medicinal note; and toasty oak ending with fine-grained tannins. Named for the vineyard bought from Duncan McRae Wood 40-plus years ago.

Food pairings: Lamb or beef in red wine sauce
Vintage years 2005, 2004, 1998

3 Tim Adams, The Fergus, Clare Valley

A full-bodied, soft-styled wine, with masses of lush raspberry and loganberry fruit dusted with Grenache spiciness and meaty, nutty flavors. Essentially Grenache grapes, with Cabernet and Shiraz in the mix, this drinks well now, but will sweeten with age.

Food pairings: Steak pie
Vintage years: 2006, 2004, 2003

5 Kilikanoon, The Oracle, Clare Valley

A company that has grown in size in just 10 years and gained quality along the way. Shiraz is the real star, with the Oracle showing its ripe, spicy, plum fruit layered with coffee, chocolate, sweet leather, and oak.

Food pairings: Prune-stuffed loin of pork
Vintage years: 2006, 2005, 2004

Adelaide Hills

Just 9 miles from the coast and at altitudes of 1,150 to 2,300 feet, this hilly area east of Adelaide is the coolest of all South Australian wine regions. Freshness and elegance are the watchwords here, with Pinot Noir the most widely planted red grape variety, although Shiraz produces intensely aromatic wines. Merlot, Sangiovese, and even Zinfandel are planted in this versatile, cool-climate region.

SOUTH AUSTRALIA

Adelaide Hills

Vines among mustard flowers, Magill, Adelaide Hills

1 Shaw and Smith, Shiraz Adelaide Hills

The Shiraz from this highly successful winery comes from a number of sites in the Adelaide Hills to reflect the region's terroir. Fragrant black cherry fruit, with a sprinkling of pepper and a dusting of cocoa, refined, and a vibrant, clean, fruity finish.

Food pairings: Lamb chops with red currant sauce
Vintage years: 2006, 2004, 2003

2 Pike and Joyce Pinot Noir, Adelaide Hills

Based in the prestigious Lenswood district, this small partnership wine business is gaining a reputation for its Pinots. Summer berry compôte notes backed by cedary oak, chocolate, and fine tannins adding backbone.

Food pairings: Grilled sea bass
Vintage years: 2007, 2006, 2005

4 Nepenthe, Tryst Red, Adelaide Hills

An adventurous winery that experiments successfully with Tempranillo and Zinfandel as well as making excellent Pinots. Tryst is a good-value, exuberant blend of Cabernet Sauvignon, Tempranillo, and Zinfandel, with bramble and cherry fruit and clean, refreshing acidity.

Food pairings: Beef-stuffed cannelloni
Vintage years 2006, 2005, 2004

3 Leabrook Estate, Three Region Shiraz, Adelaide Hills

Small boutique winery making tiny quantities of elegant wines with purity and precision. This Shiraz is Adelaide Hills fruit with a helping hand from Adelaide Plains and Langhorne Creek to add depth. Has fresh, aromatic, black fruit with clarity of style and firm, complex finish.

Food pairings: Rosemary-studded leg of lamb
Vintage years: 2005, 2004, 2003

5 Longview Devil's Elbow Cabernet Sauvignon, Adelaide Hills

Increasing quality at this growing producer, now with 200 acres of vines. Devil's Elbow is a single vineyard wine, with ripe red and black currant fruit, layers of mint, chocolate and minerals, balanced acidity, and a light touch of oak.

Food pairings: Broiled red meats
Vintage years: 2007, 2006, 2005

Fleurieu

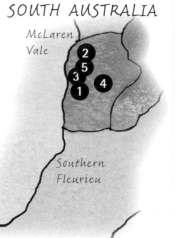

On the southern outskirts of Adelaide, competing for land with commuters and their houses, is the McLaren Vale. South Australia's first vines were planted here and the region still has many old vines. With sea breezes to keep temperatures down and the high Mount Lofty Ranges to the east, this is a versatile, productive wine region, focused mainly on reds. Here Mourvèdre, Grenache, Shiraz, and Cabernet Sauvignon produce deep, lush-flavored wines. Across the Fleurieu Peninsula, Langhorne Creek is known for its beefy reds and dessert wines, while new plantings on Kangaroo Island could prove to be the best place for Sangiovese, Cabernet Franc, and Malbec.

Vineyards in the McLaren Vale

1 Mitolo, Jester Shiraz, McLaren Vale

A fine range of wines from this producer with G.A.M. leading the Shiraz field. But this Jester Shiraz is a terrific, expressive wine with supple, intense bramble and prune fruit, laced with licorice, and ending with a sweet, ripe, showy finish.

Food pairings: Pasta dishes with beef
Vintage years: 2007, 2006, 2005

2 Coriole, Contour 4, McLaren Vale

Bursting with lively, juicy, red-cherry Sangiovese fruit, backed by the weight and succulence of great Shiraz, this wine starts out refreshing and light, then moves into darker plummy tones with chocolate and cedar on the finish. Delicious and food-friendly.

Food pairings: Hot steak sandwich with salsa
Vintage years: 2006, 2005, 2003

4 Wirra Wirra, Dead Ringer, McLaren Vale

Ripe cassis and toasty oak in this Cabernet Sauvignon wine from Wirra Wirra, which is now fully back on track. The fruit manages to be both bright and juicy as well as deep and serious, all backed up by savory, meaty notes and a strong, elegant finish.

Food pairings: Medium-rare sirloin steak
Vintage years: 2006, 2005, 2002

3 Paxton, AAA Shiraz Grenache, McLaren Vale

A ripe, generous wine, stuffed with vibrant blackberry fruit and bright peppery spice. Smoky oak is nestled among the fruit, but not enough to get in the way of the fine, savory tannins and firm, balanced finish. Organic and biodynamic methods are used here.

Food pairings: Red Thai chicken curry
Vintage years: 2006, 2004, 2002

5 D'Arenberg, Dead Arm Shiraz

With crazy names and quite substantial production, D'Arenberg still manages to keep quality high, especially in this powerful fruitcake of a wine, dense with juicy blackberry and cherry fruit, licorice, spice, and chocolate. Despite the weight of flavors, it is still balanced on the finish.

Food pairings: Grilled spare ribs
Vintage years: 2005, 2004, 2002

Limestone Coast

Once part of an ancient ocean and 180 miles south of Adelaide and more than 50 miles inland, this region is based on a subsoil of limestone ridges topped by a patchwork of soils. The most famous region, Coonawarra, has a thin, red layer of iron-rich soil known as Terra Rossa, which has helped define the area and its wines. To the north, Padthaway and Wrattonbully are still establishing their reputations, but the whole Limestone Coast is renowned for the quality of its red wines. Cabernet Sauvignon is the key grape variety, with Shiraz and Merlot also planted.

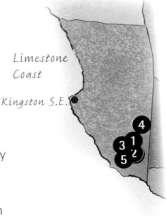

Limestone Coast

Kingston S.E.

Vineyard, Limestone Coast

① Penley Estate Phoenix Cabernet Sauvignon, Coonawarra

Kim Tolley at Penley produces rich, smooth wines across the range. This Cabernet has fragrant, ripe, blackberry fruit; a hint of spice; silky grape tannins; and elegant complexity. Full bodied, rounded, and with purity of fruit.

Food pairings: Vegetarian lasagna with tomatoes
Vintage years: 2006, 2005, 2004

② Majella, Cabernet Sauvignon, Coonawarra

Growing in size and reputation, Majella makes outstanding wines. This 100 percent Cabernet is almost black in color, with a complex nose of black currants, blueberries, and violets. The palate is rich and juicy, with plum and fruitcake characteristics, and a long, supple finish of fine-grained tannins.

Food pairings: A rich, bitter chocolate dessert
Vintage years: 2006, 2004, 2002

④ Tapanappa Whalebone Vineyard, Cabernet Shiraz, Wrattonbully

Brian Croser, formerly of Petaluma, is at the helm of this exciting new venture, based around a vineyard of old vines planted on red iron-rich soil. With ripe mulberry and blackberry fruit, silky tannins, and a harmonious, precise finish, this is an outstanding wine.

Food pairings: Roast duck breasts with cherry sauce
Vintage years: 2005, 2004, 2003

③ Reschke, Vitulus Cabernet Sauvignon, Coonawarra

Soft raspberry and blueberry aromas in this deep-colored wine. The palate has concentrated fruit with savory chocolate notes and elegant, ripe, structuring tannins. At the affordable end of Reschke range. Move up to the powerful Empyrean if the budget allows.

Food pairings: Rosemary-Parmesan polenta
Vintage years: 2005, 2004, 2002

⑤ Katnook, Prodigy, Coonawarra

Reds from this well-established, up-market producer are characterized by intense, sweet fruit. Prodigy is the premium Shiraz, with a smooth, perfumed nose, full of dark-berries with spice and sweet oak over a fleshy, muscular frame. Soft enough to drink now, with huge potential.

Food pairings: Lamb osso buco with olives
Vintage years: 2005, 2000, 1999

Victoria & Tasmania

With a climate that ranges from the heat of the Murray River to the distinct chill of the Mornington Peninsula, Victoria produces a diverse selection of wines. Shiraz does well across the whole state, from the big-volume wines of the Murray-Darling River to the vibrant fruited wines of the Grampians in the west. Coastal areas produce some of Australia's finest Pinot Noirs, while Cabernet Sauvignon ripens well in central areas. Tasmania is Australia's ultimate cool-climate region. Pinot Noir is grown extensively here, particularly for sparkling wine.

The TarraWarra estate in Yarra Valley—possibly Victoria's best premium wine area

1 Sanguine Estate, Shiraz, Heathcote

Great wines from a new estate on the red soils of Victoria's sunny, dry, Heathcote region. This is a deep-flavored wine, layered with raspberries and mulberries, a touch of mocha, and soft, spicy savoriness.

Food pairings: Moroccan-spiced lamb
Vintage years: 2006, 2005, 2004

2 Garry Crittenden Sangiovese i, King Valley

A pioneer in Victoria, Crittenden of Dromana Estate was one of the first to establish Mornington Peninsula as the place to grow Pinot. This is from his Italian varietal range with grapes sourced in northeast King Valley; savory with truffles and raspberry fruit.

Food pairings: Beef carpaccio
Vintage years: 2006, 2005, 2004

4 TarraWarra, Estate Reserve Pinot Noir, Yarra Valley

The wines gain complexity as the vines age at this stylish estate, which is totally focused on Chardonnay and Pinot Noir. This wine shows vanilla-edged raspberry fruit with a hint of spice and darker, complex notes with fine tannins.

Food pairings: Grilled mushrooms with Parmesan
Vintage years: 2006, 2005, 2004

3 De Bortoli, Shiraz Viognier, Yarra Valley

The Yarra Valley is the home of the premium part of this family-owned operation. This estate-grown Shiraz Viognier has aromas of fresh-picked violets backed by spice-dusted red berries and white pepper, with rounded, rich complexity on the palate and a long, warm finish.

Food pairings: Rabbit casserole with pearl onions
Vintage years: 2006, 2005, 2004

5 Yering Station, Reserve Shiraz Viognier, Yarra Valley

Victoria's first vineyard has been modernized with a stunning new winery and meticulous winemaking. This Reserve Shiraz has a splash of Viognier to lift the aromas; a dense palate with black cherry and plum flavors, savory notes, and a chocolate end.

Food pairings: Chocolate-dipped cherries
Vintage years: 2006, 2005, 2004

6 Kooyong Meres, Pinot Noir, Mornington Peninsula

A new estate at Tuerong at the northern end of the Mornington Peninsula. Here the drier, warmer climate ripens the fruit to give vibrant and generous cherry flavors, savory mellowness, fresh acidity, and an elegant finish.

Food pairings: Pan-fried salmon
Vintage years: 2006, 2005, 2004

7 Pirie Estate, Pinot Noir, Tasmania

From Andrew Pirie, one of the pioneers of Tasmanian wine now back in charge of his own estate, this Pinot Noir shows youthful intensity and great perfume while also having the structure to age. Clear, pure cherry and raspberry notes, with a silky, ripe texture and good length.

Food pairings: Seared scallops
Vintage years: 2006, 2005, 2004

9 Taltarni, Pyrenees Cabernet Sauvignon, Pyrenees, Victoria

This hilly region has a cooler, dry climate with a distinct nighttime drop in temperatures. The result is cleaner, fresher flavors, as in this elegant Cabernet. Changes at the winery mean fleshier wines, with good cassis fruit and a balanced, harmonious finish.

Food pairings: Venison chops with berry sauce
Vintage years: 2005, 2004, 2002

8 Tamar Ridge, Kayena Vineyard Pinot Noir, Tasmania

Based on the west bank of the Tamar River in northern Tasmania, the Tamar Ridge now has over 500 acres of vineyard and a new winery. This Pinot Noir has bright raspberry and blackberry fruit with a good balance and a complex earthy finish.

Food pairings: Roasted cod with tomato and herbs
Vintage years: 2006, 2005, 2004

10 Mount Langi Ghiran, Billi Billi, Grampians

Cooler temperatures and an afternoon breeze give wines from this property character and balance. This Billi Billi wine, made from purchased grapes, has flavor way beyond its value price. Aromatic, spicy nose; peppery, plummy fruit; and a rich, juicy finish.

Food pairings: Beef steak with green peppercorns
Vintage years: 2004, 2003, 2000

This wine cellar in Yarra Valley uses pupitres—an old technique which helps to remove sediment from the bottle caused by secondary fermentation. In this case the cellar is producing sparkling white wine

New South Wales

The Hunter Valley is the traditional home of viticulture in this state, with the focus on rich-tasting whites and supple Shiraz. In recent years the focus of attention for quality wine has shifted away from the humid lower Hunter Valley to drier climates such as those on the western slopes of the Great Dividing Range. Here, regions such as Orange provide drier and cooler climates for grapes. Even Canberra District is now growing in interest and quality, whereas the hot, central Riverina District has been a bulk producer of wine for many years.

An old Shiraz vine grows at Tyrell's Wines, Hunter Valley

1 Brokenwood, Graveyard Vineyard Shiraz, Hunter Valley

With floods wiping out the 2008 vintage from this benchmark winery in the lower Hunter Valley, demand for this wine is bound to be high. Dense, purple, intense fruit, with plum and spice to the fore, and grippy tannins that will need several years to mellow.

Food pairings: Pheasant casserole
Vintage years: 2006, 2005, 2002

2 Tyrrell's Winemaker Selection Vat 8, Hunter Valley

Still family-owned after nearly 150 years, Tyrrell's makes this Shiraz Cabernet blend at its original heartland in the Hunter Valley. It has deep, savory fruit; earthy complexity, balanced with good acidity; and a meaty, long finish.

Food pairings: Braised beef in red wine
Vintage years: 2006, 2004, 2002

4 Clonakilla, Hilltops Shiraz, Canberra District

A small family winery making distinctive, handcrafted wines. Drink the exceptional Shiraz Viognier when you can find it, but this is more affordable and available, with powerful, peppery, red fruits; chocolate, a touch of licorice, and firm, structuring tannins.

Food pairings: Prune-stuffed loin of pork
Vintage years: 2006, 2005, 2004

3 De Bortoli, Show Liqueur Muscat, Riverina

The traditional non-vintage wine from this hot region. Grapes are left on the vines long after normal ripening, fermented, fortified to 18 percent and then aged. This is fruitcake in a glass, with rich coffee, figs, and toffee on the palate.

Food pairings: Baked apples in maple syrup
Vintage years: NV

5 Cumulus Climbing Merlot, Orange

This is one of Australia's highest vineyards, a massive 1,250 acres at altitude on the slopes of the Central Dividing Range, 150 miles west of Sydney. Cool temperatures and bright sunshine produce vibrant, intense berry fruit with cool-climate leafiness and balanced acidity.

Food pairings: Tagliatelle with basil pesto
Vintage years: 2006, 2005, 2004

Western Australia

What Western Australia lacks in quantity, it makes up for in quality. Vineyards here produce around 20 percent of the country's premium wines from just 4 percent of the total volume. Margaret River is the focus of attention, with not just vines, but a great maritime-influenced climate and the surf of the ocean just a short drive away. Ripe, elegant, structured Cabernet Sauvignons are the real stars, though there are excellent Merlots, Shiraz, and good red blends. The surrounding areas of Geographe, Manjimup, and Pemberton are growing in importance.

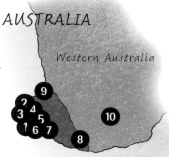

Cape Mentelle Vineyard, Margaret River

1 Cape Mentelle, Cabernet Sauvignon, Margaret River

Good quality from one of Margaret River's leading producers. Concentrated, structured, and cedary, with scents of herbs, black currant, mulberry, and chocolate, and layers of cherries, currants, mocha, and tobacco on the palate. For a rare Australian taste, try Cape Mentelle Zinfandel.

Food pairings: Herb-crusted rack of lamb
Vintage years: 2004, 2003, 2001

2 Vasse Felix, Cabernet Sauvignon, Margaret River

This was the first commercial vineyard established in Margaret River 40 years ago, and the quality has remained high. Pure, clear, cassis fruit shines out on the nose; the palate has a silky weight and savory, cedary notes with balance, elegance, and length.

Food pairings: Rosemary-studded roast lamb
Vintage years: 2005, 2003, 2001

4 Cullen, Mangan, Margaret River

An unusual blend of Merlot, Petit Verdot, and Malbec from a single vineyard, where low yields and a biodynamic approach produce deep-flavored characterful wines. This has rich plum and blackberry fruit, with a light herbal note and soft, plush tannins.

Food pairings: Broiled calves' liver with onions
Vintage years: 2006, 2005, 2002

3 Moss Wood, Cabernet Sauvignon, Margaret River

Handcrafted wines with superb depth at this small company. The fruit is deep, ripe, and opulent in an understated way. Mulberries, cassis, and chocolate are all in the mix, but it is best understood as a complex, satisfying whole, still with years to evolve into a stunning wine.

Food pairings: Top quality mature cheese
Vintage years: 2005, 2004, 2000

5 Stella Bella, Cabernet Merlot, Margaret River

Within a trio of memorable labels—Stella Bella, Suckfizzle, and Skuttlebutt—McDonald and Pym pack in all the powerful fruit and variety possible. Rich in red currant, mulberries, and brambly fruit, this has lush flavors within a classic structure.

Food pairings: Bacon-wrapped roasted chicken
Vintage years: 2006, 2005, 2002

6 Voyager Estate, Shiraz, Margaret River

Great quality at this meticulous estate. The Shiraz is fermented with a splash of Viognier in open fermenters, which lends perfumed, floral notes to the aromas of black cherry fruit and dense, ripe, peppery, plummy flavors.

Food pairings: Beef lasagna
Vintage years: 2006, 2005, 2004

7 Leeuwin Estate Art Series Cabernet Sauvignon

One of the best properties in Margaret River, Leeuwin Estate wines have finesse and elegance. This Cabernet shows ripe, intense blackberry and mulberry fruit with touches of spice and dark chocolate, followed by silky, smooth tannins.

Food pairings: Broiled lamb chops with thyme
Vintage years: 2004, 2003, 2001

9 Capel Vale Shiraz Debut, Western Australia

Capel Vale has vineyards across Margaret River, Mount Barker, and Pemberton. Debut is easy-drinking, full of fruit range, packing red berry and black pepper fruit with lively aromas and silky texture. Trade up to Mount Barker Shiraz for deeper flavors.

Food pairings: Broiled steak and salad
Vintage years: 2007, 2006, 2005

8 Fonty's Pool Shiraz, Pemberton

Southeast of Margaret River, with vineyards in Manjimup, this brand is owned by Cape Mentelle, producing impressive wines at affordable prices. This Shiraz has precise red berry and plum fruit; a streak of light, integrated spice; and a balanced, long finish.

Food pairings: Tuna with roasted red peppers
Vintage years: 2006, 2005, 2003

10 Alkoomi Black Label Shiraz Viognier, Frankland River

Alkoomi is aboriginal for "a place we choose"—the Lange family chose to plant their 255 acres of vines in Frankland River, where afternoon sea breezes moderate daytime temperatures. This wine has ripe cherry and raspberry fruit with fine, structuring tannins.

Food pairings: Mushroom and eggplant lasagna
Vintage years: 2007, 2006, 2005

6   7   8   9   10

The sun sets over Cape Mentelle vineyard in Margaret River

NEW ZEALAND

Auckland

Hawkes Bay

Wairarapa
Wellington

Marlborough

Christchurch

Central Otago

New Zealand

New Zealand's fame for crisp, zesty whites and dusky, fruity reds has developed only in the last 20 years. Sauvignon Blanc was the first wine to really put New Zealand on the map, but now it is the reds, in particular Pinot Noir, which are sought out around the world for their food-friendly fruitiness. New Zealand has a cool climate. Surrounded by the sea with icy Antarctic currents sweeping up its coasts, combined with strong winds bringing rain to the west coast, the main wine-growing regions are in protected areas, mostly on the eastern side of the islands.

The first vineyards were planted on the North Island in the Auckland area. The city remains the center of the wine trade because major producers have their offices and, in some cases, their bottling plants there. However, vineyards have spread out across the North and South Island and extend 700 miles south to Central Otago, the most southerly vineyards in the world.

On the North Island, particularly on the eastern coast around Hawkes Bay, Merlot, Cabernet Sauvignon, and Syrah are becoming success stories, producing rich, fruity, fresh-tasting wines. At the North Island's southern end, the region of Wairarapa has gained a reputation for its Pinot Noir. Across the Cook Strait in the northern part of the South Island, Marlborough has become world-famous for its Sauvignon Blanc, but these stony soils also ripen Pinot Noir well. Farther south, in the region of Central Otago, protected by mountains from the coastal influence, Pinot Noir is capable of producing wines that rival Burgundy for their vibrant, complex flavors.

Hawkes Bay

On the sheltered east coast of the North Island, Hawkes Bay is New Zealand's second-largest wine region. With consistent, reliable sunshine, warm summers, and dry falls, this is the country's leading red wine area with Merlot, Cabernet Sauvignon, Malbec, and, increasingly, Syrah as the most important varieties. Soil types vary across the region, from wide alluvial plains to limestone hillsides, but one area, the deep stony soil of the Gimblett Gravels district, has been identified as an area for high-quality wines.

Barrique cellar in Te Mata Estate, Havelock North, Hawkes Bay

1 Esk Valley Reserve, Merlot/Cabernet Sauvignon/Malbec, Hawkes Bay

Esk is part of the Villa Maria group, and winemaker Gordon Russell makes particularly good reds. Grapes come from the Gimblett Gravels district and, after a long maceration in open-top fermenters, provide lush, smooth, blackberry and raspberry fruit with fine-grained tannins.

Food pairings: Broiled lamb chops
Vintage years: 2005, 2004, 2002

2 Villa Maria Private Bin, Merlot Cabernet Sauvignon, Hawkes Bay

This is the good introductory level in the Villa Maria range. It is full of black currant fruit and tobacco notes, with herb-edged tannins and a long finish. Trade up to Reserve for substantially more complexity and finesse.

Food pairings: Mushroom risotto or lasagna
Vintage years: 2007, 2006, 2005

4 Craggy Range, Le Sol, Hawkes Bay

This dynamic company has an obsessive approach to quality viticulture, carefully matching soil type to variety. The winemaking is good too. Le Sol is the top-level Syrah with peppery, blackberry aromas, opulent fruit, and a smooth, classy finish.

Food pairings: Beef Wellington
Vintage years: 2006, 2005, 2004

3 Te Mata, Coleraine, Hawkes Bay

One of New Zealand's most outstanding red wines with the ability to age and develop complexity. A Cabernet Sauvignon, Merlot, and Cabernet Franc blend with a concentrated, dark-crimson color, complex black currant and spiced plum fruit, and ripe, structuring tannins.

Food pairings: Braised oxtail with red wine
Vintage years: 2006, 2005, 2003

5 Trinity Hill, Syrah, Hawkes Bay

Consistent, quality wines across the range here, in particular this Syrah from Gimblett Gravels Road. There is just a splash of Viognier to lift the aroma, and the palate is rich with blackberry, black pepper, and savory and spicy flavors, with a distinct Rhône-like character.

Food pairings: Beef casserole
Vintage years: 2007, 2006, 2003

Wairarapa

At the southern tip of the North Island, protected from the prevailing wind and rain by a small range of hills, the region of Wairarapa has become famous for Pinot Noir. Its dry, sunny climate with warm days and chilly nights, combined with free-draining gravelly river terraces, provides the ideal conditions for developing top-quality, complex wines. Most producers in this region are boutique establishments, making limited quantities of handcrafted wines. The small town of Martinborough is where many of the producers are based.

The well-established Martinborough Vineyard in Wairarapa

1 Ata Rangi, Pinot Noir, Martinborough, Wairarapa

One of the pioneers in Martinborough, Clive Paton now has some of the oldest vines in the region. Low yields and open canopies allow full ripening of the grapes to produce savory, silky-textured wines with dark-cherry tones and a rich, long finish.

Food pairings: Slow-cooked lamb with lentils
Vintage years: 2006, 2005, 2003

2 Schubert, Pinot Noir "Block B," Wairarapa

Kai Schubert and Marion Deimling left their native Germany to find the most interesting place to plant Pinot Noir—Wairarapa. Even with young vines, the wines are exciting, with aromas of ripe, dark cherries, soft aromatic fruit, and silky tannins.

Food pairings: Veal with red wine sauce
Vintage years: 2007, 2006, 2004

4 Escarpment Kupe, Pinot Noir, Martinborough

Larry McKenna, once at Martinborough Vineyard, now has his own vineyard on the gravel soil of Te Muna Ridge. Close-planted vines, low yields, and meticulous winemaking have produced this concentrated, deep-flavored, rich-textured wine.

Food pairings: Braised pheasant with bacon
Vintage years: 2006, 2005, 2003

3 Martinborough Vineyard, Pinot Noir, Martinborough

The fruit quality has always been good at this well-established property. Clear raspberry and strawberry fruit lead into more earthy flavors, good complexity, and a warm, mulberry-soaked finish.

Food pairings: Baked sea bass
Vintage years: 2006, 2005, 2004

5 Murdoch James Estate, Saleyards Syrah, Martinborough

This is one of the few Syrahs from this marginal climate, but Murdoch James, who farm organically, manage to pack serious white pepper, herbs, and savory notes among the damson and cassis fruit. Keep this wine three to six years.

Food pairings: Steak with Parmesan-topped mushrooms
Vintage years: 2006, 2004, 2003

Marlborough

Marlborough is New Zealand's largest wine-growing area with a reputation for some vibrant Sauvignon Blancs. Pinot Noir is increasingly being planted in this region, making the most of the abundant sunshine, cool nights, and a long ripening season to produce elegant, fruity wines. The region is based around the stony soils of the Wairau Valley, although the later-ripening Awatere Valley and the slopes of the Southern Valley are proving particularly suitable for Pinot Noir.

SOUTH ISLAND

Marlborough

The slopes of the Southern Valley above vineyards in Marlborough

1 Delta Vineyard "Hatters Hill" Pinot Noir, Marlborough

This new vineyard, planted on clay-rich slopes at the mouth of the Waihopai Valley, is producing astonishingly good wine for such young vines. Soft and elegant with lifted cherry aromas, savory complexity, and a supple, clean, raspberry-edged finish.

Food pairings: Herb-coated pork chops
Vintage years: 2007, 2006, 2005

2 Villa Maria, Taylors Pass Pinot Noir, Marlborough

From the warm, stony, rugged terrain of Taylors Pass Vineyard in Awatere Valley, this wine has layers of concentrated dark fruits with a long, silky texture and an elegant, balanced, stylish finish.

Food pairings: Rosemary-scented leg of lamb
Vintage years: 2007, 2006, 2005

4 Cloudy Bay, Pinot Noir, Marlborough

With a range of top-quality Pinot Noir clones planted in the warmer soils of Benmorven, Brancott, and Omaka Valleys, grapes for this wine are now reaching complete ripeness. The result is clear black cherry fruit, with layers of spice and a velvety, elegant finish.

Food pairings: Broiled salmon with fennel
Vintage years: 2006, 2005, 2004

3 Wither Hills, Pinot Noir, Marlborough

Dark, savory fruit with plums and red berries, a weighty palate, and soft, subtle tannins make this one of the more elegant Pinots from Marlborough. The winemaker has now moved on; will quality remain the same?

Food pairings: Baked cod with herbs
Vintage years: 2007, 2006, 2005

5 Saint Clair Doctor's Creek, Pinot Noir, Marlborough

Growing rapidly in size and reputation, Saint Clair produces a fine range from simple varieties to site-specific wines. This is a rounded luscious Pinot, with red currant and cherry fruit balanced by warm, savory oak notes and a long finish.

Food pairings: Spinach and vegetable tarts
Vintage years: 2007, 2006, 2005

Central Otago

These are the most southerly vineyards in the world and quite probably the most beautiful. Situated in the rain shadow of the Southern Alps, at between 900 and 1,200 feet altitude, this region is protected from coastal influences and has a continental climate with cold winters and warm, dry summers. The large variation in temperature between day and night during the ripening period leads to intense flavors and depth of color in the skins—perfect for Pinot Noir. Almost 80 percent of the vineyard area is devoted to Pinot Noir.

Queenstown

5
2
3
4
1

Central Otago

Rippon Vineyard in winter, Wanaka, Central Otago

1 Felton Road, Pinot Noir, Central Otago

Ungrafted vines, biodynamic viticulture, and small-scale winemaking make the wines from this property some of the most handcrafted wines from Otago. Cherry and wild thyme combine on the aroma, leading to dense, complex, herb-strewn fruit, and a structured, firm palate. This needs time.

Food pairings: Broiled lamb steaks
Vintage years: 2007, 2006, 2005

2 Quartz Reef, Pinot Noir, Central Otago

With vineyards on a perfect north-facing slope in Bendigo, winemaker Rudi Bauer builds layers of flavor in his wines. This Pinot Noir has a succulent expression of cherry and plum fruit backed by firm, silky tannins and savory meatiness. Needs time to open up.

Food pairings: Seared tuna with chanterelles
Vintage years: 2007, 2006, 2005

4 Carrick, Unravelled Pinot Noir, Central Otago

Seaweed is the latest compost material at this environmentally aware vineyard on the gravelly, sandy soil in the warm area of Bannockburn. The wine has ripe plum and cherry fruit with spice, cedary oak, and balanced acidity on the finish.

Food pairings: Broiled salmon with lentils
Vintage years: 2006, 2005, 2002

3 Mt Difficulty, Roaring Meg Pinot Noir, Central Otago

This affordable and accessible wine comes from the prestigious Mt Difficulty Winery. While it does not pretend to be a match for the main wine, it has the right raspberry fruit, with savory notes, a touch of licorice, and a firm, structured finish.

Food pairings: Spiced lamb tagine
Vintage years: 2007, 2006, 2004

5 Rippon, Pinot Noir, Central Otago

Overlooking Lake Wanaka, with a backdrop of snowcapped mountains, Rippon is surely the most beautiful vineyard in the world. Proprietor Nick Mills worked in Burgundy for several years, and this shows in the wine, with its complexity, density, and sheer effortless quality.

Food pairings: Duck breast with truffles
Vintage years: 2006, 2005, 2002

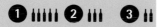

1 ⅠⅠⅠⅠⅠ 2 ⅠⅠⅠ 3 ⅠⅠ   4 ⅠⅠⅠ 5 ⅠⅠⅠⅠⅠ

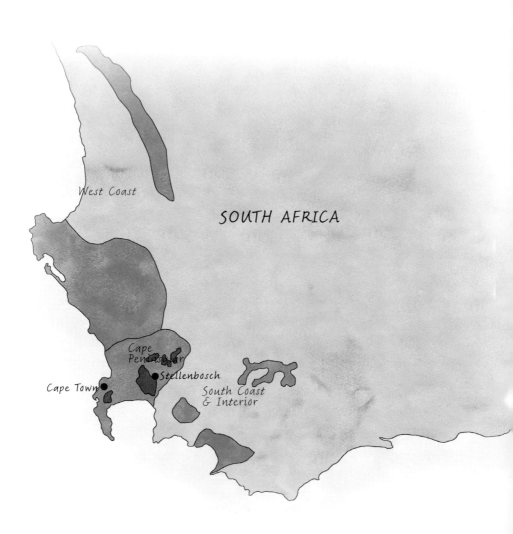

West Coast

SOUTH AFRICA

Cape
Peninsula

Cape Town • Stellenbosch

South Coast
& Interior

South Africa

We may think of South Africa as a relatively New World producer, but it has been making wine for over 350 years and now ranks as the eighth-largest wine producer in the world. The first European settlers at the Cape established a supply station for ships on their way to the Orient. They planted vines and within a short period of time the sweet wines of Constantia had become some of the most expensive and sought-after wines in Europe.

But it has not been an easy ride for South African wines. Trade tariffs in the eighteenth century, vine disease in the nineteenth century, and long years of isolation in the twentieth century meant that when South Africa opened up for business just two decades ago there was a lot of catching up to do. Vineyards were planted with the wrong varieties and winemaking had been held back by lack of investment. All this has now changed, along with fresh enthusiasm and huge investment in the vineyards and new wineries.

Most vineyards are in the southwest of the country, centered around Stellenbosch, just outside Cape Town, and they spread out along the cool coastline and into the heat of the interior. This is essentially a Mediterranean climate—warm and sunny, with rain falling in winter. The soil is rich and varied, with several mountain ranges creating microclimates for specific varieties and wine styles. Grape varieties include the usual international styles; however, Pinotage, a crossing of Pinot Noir and Cinsault, is widely planted, producing distinctive, deep-flavored red wines.

Cape Peninsula

The heartland of South Africa's wine industry—the Coastal Region—includes Stellenbosch, the historic center of the Winelands. About 30 miles east of Cape Town, just 7 miles inland and almost 1,000 feet above sea level, this fertile area produces quality red wines from the rugged sandstone and granite soils. To the north, Paarl is slightly warmer, giving richer Shiraz and Merlots, while Franschhoek, possibly the most dramatic and beautiful of South Africa's wine regions, is at a higher, cooler altitude, providing refined Cabernets and Shiraz. Constantia and Cape Point are cool districts where reds are beginning to develop.

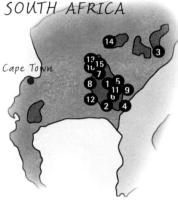

Pinotage grapes in South Africa have a youthful flavor: full and ripe

① Rustenberg, John X Merriman, Stellenbosch

Vines on the sheltered southwest slopes of the Simonsberg Mountains provide the grapes for this Bordeaux blend of Cabernet Sauvignon and Merlot. Thirteen percent Petit Verdot adds aromatic generosity to the seamless, sleek, structured cassis and bittersweet chocolate flavors.

Food pairings: Broiled lamb chops
Vintage years: 2006, 2004, 2003

② Ken Forrester, Petit Pinotage, Coastal Region

Restaurateur and grape-grower Ken Forrester makes stunning Chenin Blanc, but his Pinotage is also good. Petit Pinotage is a youthful style of this grape —deep, inky red in color, and full of ripe, juicy mulberry fruit with an edge of herbs and tannin.

Food pairings: Grilled ribs or pizza
Vintage years: 2007, 2006

④ Vergelegen Red, Stellenbosch

Vergelegen's exceptional winemaker, Andre van Rensburg, produces a fine range of wines including this Cabernet Sauvignon–dominated Bordeaux blend with silky, supple, sweet red-berried fruit; cedar-edged complexity; and a long, balanced finish. It shows well when young, but deserves five years in bottle.

Food pairings: Herbed rack of lamb
Vintage years: 2004, 2003, 2000

③ Boekenhoutskloof, The Chocolate Block, Western Cape

Stylish wines from Marc Kent across the range from this Franschhoek-based farm, but this Syrah-led blend is sourced from key vineyards across the Cape. It has rich-flavored, chocolate-spiced, dark berry fruit, with smooth tannins and the ability to age.

Food pairings: Roast beef
Vintage years: 2006, 2005, 2004

⑤ Tokara Red, Stellenbosch

Stylish wines across the range from this high-tech winery. The Red, a Cabernet Sauvignon, Merlot, and Petit Verdot blend sourced from vineyards on the slopes of the Simonsberg Mountains, has blackberry and pencil-shaving complexity with a silky, textured finish.

Food pairings: Herb-crusted venison with sautéed potatoes
Vintage years: 2005, 2004, 2003

6 Ernie Els, Meritage, Stellenbosch 🛢

Champion golf pro Ernie Els is part-owner here and as much work goes into the wines as into his swing. This Cabernet-dominated Bordeaux blend presents pure, fresh cassis and red currant fruit, with vanilla, spice, and a seamless tannin structure.

Food pairings: Rack of lamb
Vintage years: 2006, 2005, 2004

7 Beyerskloof Cape Blend, Stellenbosch

Depth of flavor and complexity are the main strength of Beyers Truter's wines. Vines for this Cape Blend of Cabernet Sauvignon, Pinotage, and Merlot are close-planted and produce dark black currant and cassis flavors with smooth, integrated tannins.

Food pairings: Grilled red meat
Vintage years: 2005, 2004, 2002

9 Thelema The Mint Cabernet Sauvignon, Stellenbosch

Consistent high quality from this stunning mountainside property. Grapes for The Mint come from a single clone of old Cabernet vines, which have a distinct minty scent among ripe cassis flavors. Twenty months of aging in new French oak make this elegant and age-worthy.

Food pairings: Medium-rare beef
Vintage years: 2006, 2005, 2004

8 Jordan/Jardin Cobblers Hill Cabernet Sauvignon, Stellenbosch

The Jordan's wines are known as Jardin in the States, but the flavors are still majestic, rounded, complex, and elegant. This age-worthy blend of Cabernet Sauvignon, Merlot, and Cabernet Franc comes from top-quality vineyards and spends two years in French oak.

Food pairings: Roast pork with sweet potatoes
Vintage years: 2005, 2004, 2003

10 Kanonkop Pinotage, Stellenbosch

Johann and Paul Krige wait until absolute ripeness before picking the Pinotage. Then hand-sorting of the grapes, hand-plunging of the fermentation vats, and 16 months in mainly new oak give deep, spice-laden flavors with a restrained but positive tannic structure.

Food pairings: Grilled meats, hamburgers with spicy salsas
Vintage years: 2006, 2005, 2004

The view overlooking Jordan Vineyards, Stellenbosch

Destemming at the Rustenberg Estate—here grapes are sorted for quality

11 Rust en Vrede Merlot, Stellenbosch

Established in 1694 and owned by the Engelbrecht family for the last 30 years, this historic estate has built a fine reputation for its wines. Only reds are produced here, including this fleshy, sumptuous Merlot with savory notes and velvety tannins.

Food pairings: Broiled red meats or vegetarian chili
Vintage years: 2006, 2004, 2003

12 Meerlust Rubicon, Stellenbosch

The cooling effect of the Atlantic, just three miles southwest of this historic property, ensures slow ripening and dense flavors. Rubicon, the flagship wine, is a Cabernet Sauvignon–dominated Bordeaux blend with expressive blackberry fruit, smoky oak, and spices on the finish.

Food pairings: Venison with berry sauce
Vintage years: 2004, 2003, 2001

14 Goats do Roam, "Goat Roti," Coastal Region

Chuckle over the impertinence of the wine names from this offshoot company at Charles Back's Fairview, but taste the flavors too. Syrah with a dash of Viognier gives violets on the nose, smoky dark fruit on the palate, and a chocolaty finish.

Food pairings: Chicken curry
Vintage years: 2007, 2005, 2004

13 Warwick Trilogy, Stellenbosch

Cabernet Sauvignon dominates the blend from this hillside estate. After two years in French oak, it emerges closed and tight-knit, but a few years in bottle allow the rich cassis and spice flavors to emerge in perfect harmony with the structure.

Food pairings: Roast quail
Vintage years: 2005, 2004, 2003

15 Simonsig Estate Merindol, Stellenbosch

A single vineyard 100 percent Syrah wine from this quality estate's weathered granite and clay soil. Extended maceration gives a deep color with aromas of white pepper and licorice; lush, ripe mulberry and plum fruit; and velvety smooth tannins.

Food pairings: Grilled white fish served with tomatoes and mushrooms
Vintage years: 2005, 2004, 2001

West Coast

Occupying a vast area of rolling countryside, the Swartland District is home to wheatfields, vineyards, and large wine cooperatives. But this area is showing real potential as small producers select pockets of land for quality production. Untrellised bush vines produce a low crop and yield powerful, dense-flavored Shiraz, Cabernet, and Pinotage wines. Farther north the Olifants River region is also discovering its quality zones. To the east, the cool hills of Cederberg produce refined and sleek wines, while the mountainous Tulbagh District is acquiring a reputation for its quality reds.

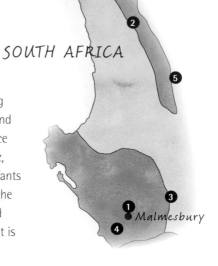

Olifants River

SOUTH AFRICA

Malmesbury

Hand picking grapes is considered the best—it minimizes damage and allows for greater selectivity

1 Sequillo Cellars, Sequillo Red, Swartland

Unirrigated old bush vines have made this a premium area in recent years. Eben Sadie makes outstanding wines. This is the affordable range, a Syrah, Mourvèdre, and Grenache blend with warm and generous fruit, herbs, power, and supple tannins.

Food pairings: Roasted red meats such as beef steaks or hamburgers
Vintage years: 2006, 2005, 2004

2 Stellar Organics Winery Cabernet Sauvignon, Olifants River

Organic production, biodiversity in the vineyards, and Fairtrade too, which means that everyone shares in the profits. And the wines taste good, too. Soft, ripe, juicy cassis and minty fruit, easy on tannins, and instantly enjoyable.

Food pairings: Simple pizzas and pasta dishes
Vintage years: 2008, 2007, 2006

4 Spice Route Flagship Syrah, Swartland

Dry-farmed, low-yielding vines on the clay slopes near Malmesbury provide the grapes for this wine. Hand punch-downs, basket pressing, and 18 months of French oak give the wine opulent black plum fruit, with savory spice and layers of flavor.

Food pairings: Oregano-flavored dishes such as chicken cacciatore
Vintage years: 2005, 2004, 2003

3 Tulbagh Mountain Vineyards Viktoria, Western Cape

From the mountain slopes of Tulbagh at 1,200 feet altitude where cool nighttime temperatures allow slower ripening and more intense flavors, this Shiraz-dominated blend has spice and fruit on the nose with a velvety, juicy palate.

Food pairings: Grilled pork shoulder
Vintage years: 2005, 2004

5 Cederberg Cabernet Sauvignon, Olifants River

South Africa's highest altitude vineyards provide grapes for these wines in the middle of a biodiversity conservation area within Cederberg. Focused cassis and black fruit with spiced mint within a broad, supple tannic structure.

Food pairings: Pepper-rubbed rib roast
Vintage years: 2006, 2005, 2004

South Coast & Interior

East of Stellenbosch, the cool upland region of Elgin is mainly a white wine area, but it is starting to produce some exciting, elegant reds, particularly Shiraz and Pinot. Closer to the coast are Walker Bay and the sheltered, undulating land of the Hemel-en-Aarde Valley. This is probably the best place in South Africa to grow quality Pinot Noir. (The high ridge separating the vineyards from the sea is also the best place to watch whales come into the bay.) To the east, the Elim is just starting to get promising results with red grapes, while farther north and inland, Worcester and Robertson are the source of improving commercial wines.

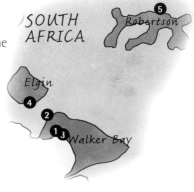

This vineyard near Robertson grows mainly white grapes, but red are becoming increasingly popular

1 Bouchard Finlayson Hannibal, Walker Bay

Peter Finlayson's main focus is on his superb Pinot Noirs, but this eclectic blend of Sangiovese, Pinot Noir, Nebbiolo, Barbera, and Shiraz provides well-knit flavors of earthy, spicy fruit with minerally undertones, balanced by clean, lively acidity. A good food wine.

Food pairings: Mildly spiced pork and vegetarian dishes
Vintage years: 2006, 2005

2 Niels Verburg Shiraz, Walker Bay

The focus is on Shiraz at this small property on the cool southeastern slopes of the Houw Hoek Mountains just 20 miles from the Atlantic. It is deep-colored, rich with plums and chocolate-coated raspberry flavors, and layered with spice, with fine, structuring tannins.

Food pairings: Lightly spiced chicken curry
Vintage years: 2005, 2004, 2003

4 Paul Cluver Pinot Noir, Elgin

Making the most of its cool, elevated Elgin position, Pinot Noir ripens well on this environmentally run estate. This Pinot Noir has aromatic strawberry and cherry fruit, underpinned by earthy notes, with mocha toastiness and soft tannins.

Food pairings: Grilled white fish with herbs
Vintage years: 2007, 2006, 2004

3 Hamilton Russell Pinot Noir, Walker Bay

Pinot Noir is the only red grape planted on this manicured estate just a hilltop ridge away from the sea. Meticulous winemaking brings perfumed red and black cherry fruit, layered with sweet spice and mineral notes, and a long, silky, persistent, elegant finish.

Food pairings: Lamb baked with aromatic herbs, like lavender
Vintage years: 2007, 2005, 2005

5 Springfield, Work of Time, Robertson

Consistent quality from this estate, mainly for whites, but this Merlot-dominated Bordeaux blend does well on the chalky soil, producing lively, bright cassis and red currant fruit, chocolate, and spice with a touch of oak.

Food pairings: Chicken casserole
Vintage years: 2003, 2002, 2001

Champagne

Alsace

Chablis

● Paris

Loire

FRANCE

Burgundy

Jura &
Savoie

Beaujolais

Bordeaux

The Dordogne

Bordeaux ●

The Rhone

Southwest

Provence

Toulouse ●

Languedoc

Marseille ●

Roussillon

France

France is the most important wine-producing country in the world. Not only does it vie with Italy for the top production slot, but it also produces the most famous wines—Champagne, Bordeaux, Burgundy, and Rhône—which set benchmarks for winemakers around the world.

This fame has not come easily. For over 2,000 years the vineyards of France have survived invasion, wars, vine disease, and economic slumps. Even now some regions are under threat because of wine imports from around the world. Over the years the best sites have been selected and nurtured to create harmony between vines and the land. Grape varieties have been chosen (and jealously guarded) to create regional characteristics and flavors. It is only because red Bordeaux is dependent on blends of Cabernet Sauvignon, Merlot, and Cabernet Franc that the region presents such a cohesive image to the world. The same applies to red Burgundy, a beacon of excellence for Pinot Noir lovers.

France has a wide variety of sites, from the cool north where Pinot Noir and Chardonnay combine to produce elegant Champagne, to the warm south where varieties such as Syrah, Grenache, and Mourvèdre hide behind seemingly ordinary Vins de Pays labels, though their strength, power, and flavor demonstrate their true quality.

France's wine laws are the most comprehensive in the world, setting out wine names, yields, and permitted grape varieties. Appellation d'Origine Contrôlée (AC) is the top classification, with a broader, less restrictive Vins de Pays (VdP) category for other wines. Within an AC there may be further ranking of quality.

Bordeaux

Situated on the Gironde Estuary in southwest France, Bordeaux is the largest producer of fine wine in France. With 300,000 acres of vines, this is a powerhouse of production, not just providing the top 100 world-famous names, but regular-drinking Bordeaux wines too.

Located close to the Atlantic and with rivers running through it, Bordeaux has a stable maritime climate, but this also provides its greatest challenge. Variable weather during June can sometimes disrupt flowering, so a range of grape varieties that flower during different weeks offers some insurance against the weather. The same goes for ripening. Cabernet Sauvignon provides structure, backbone, and flavor to the wines, but it ripens later than the soft velvety Merlot, so a prudent grower has a balance of varieties. Cabernet Franc adds aroma to the wines, while Petit Verdot, planted in tiny proportions, adds top-notes of aroma and flavor.

The gravelly soils of the Left Bank are most suited to Cabernet Sauvignon, producing fine, elegant wines, but as the proportion of gravel falls toward the northern Médoc, more Merlot is planted, which can ripen in the cold, clay soils. On the Right Bank, the clay and limestone soils are ideally suited to Merlot. Vintages are important in Bordeaux, as the climate of one year can have a dramatic effect on wine style and quality.

❶ Médoc

❷ Pomerol

❸ Graves

❹ St Emilion

❺ Bordeaux Côtes

BORDEAUX

Bordeaux's position on the
west coast of France, together
with its unique soil structures
and long history of wine
production have helped
make it the most important
quality wine production area
in France.

Médoc and Graves

The Médoc may be the most famous strip of vineyard in the world. From the north of the estuary, clay is dominant in the soil (good for Merlot), while farther south the proportion of gravel increases, allowing Cabernet Sauvignon to put down its roots. In Graves, the name says it all. This is gravelly soil, farther from the estuary, where both reds and whites do well. The wines of this region were classified in 1855, and the classification still stands almost unchanged. Top wines, known as Crus ("growths"), are the world's leading wines. Wines outside this classification often are better value.

BORDEAUX

Médoc

Haut-Médoc

Bordeaux

Graves

The grand wine cellar of Château Margaux

1 Château d'Angludet, Margaux

Much more a family home than a grand château, this property has 80 acres of carefully managed, 25-year-old Cabernet Sauvignon, Merlot, and Petit Verdot vines. The wine has gentle berry fruit with cedary edges and a polished sheen of quality.

Food pairings: Rosemary-seasoned leg of lamb
Vintage years: 2005, 2004, 2000

2 Château Kirwan, Margaux

This third-growth 88-acre property has seen a change in style since consultant Michel Rolland took an interest. Crushed blackberry fruit and cigar-box aromas with licorice, coffee, and vanilla on the palate and silky textured tannins.

Food pairings: Braised beef in red wine
Vintage years: 2006, 2003, 1999

4 Château Haut-Bages-Liberal, Pauillac

The vineyards of this property are next to the famous Château Latour, and the capable winemaking skills of Claire Villars create a deep, dark wine, full of plum and black currant fruit with cigar-box perfume and silky tannins.

Food pairings: Spring lamb, pink and juicy
Vintage years: 2005, 2002, 2001

3 Château Prieuré Lichine, Margaux

Previously owned by American Alexis Lichine, this 170-acre property lost quality for a while but is now making a comeback with consultant Stéphane Derencourt in charge. Impressive floral style, with ripe red fruits and solid concentration.

Food pairings: Chicken or rabbit in red wine
Vintage years: 2006, 2005, 2000

5 Château Pontet-Canet, Pauillac

There has been recent dramatic improvement in quality here as the balance of grapes has changed to include more Merlot in the blend. It still needs five years aging, but then its black currant fruit and concentrated, chewy flavors emerge with elegance.

Food pairings: Standing rib roast
Vintage years: 2005, 2002, 1996

1 🍾🍾🍾🍾 2 🍾🍾🍾🍾🍾 3 🍾🍾🍾 4 🍾🍾🍾🍾 5 🍾🍾🍾🍾

6 Château Les Ormes de Pez, St Estèphe

Serious Cabernet Sauvignon–dominated claret at an affordable price from this 86-acre estate. Full, chewy, black currant and cherry fruit, with raisins and spicy notes, touches of cedar box, and ripe, supple tannins.

Food pairings: Sausages with potatoes and onion gravy
Vintage years: 2005, 2003, 2000

7 Château Smith Haut Lafitte, Pessac-Léognan

A change in ownership has brought massive investment at this property, which not only makes wine but also has a hotel and a wine-therapy spa. Good depth of flavor in the wine now, with serious structure; firm, ripe fruit; and a savory finish.

Food pairings: Medium-rare beef rib
Vintage years: 2006, 2005, 2003

9 Clos du Marquis, St Julien

Château Léoville Las Cases is sensational with abundant fruit and layers of pencil shavings, licorice, and chocolate complexity. To maintain this quality, up to half of the top wine is consigned to the second label, Clos du Marquis. It is a bargain.

Food pairings: Roast loin of lamb, pink in the middle
Vintage years: 2005, 2000, 1998

8 Château Léoville Barton, St Julien

This 120-acre second-growth estate under Anthony Barton's guidance has become one of the Médoc stars. Supremely elegant, with weighty, opulent blackberry and bilberry fruit and structuring tannins, it needs 10 years to emerge as sleek as a racehorse.

Food pairings: Herb-crusted rack of lamb
Vintage years: 2005, 2000, 1998

10 Château Ducru-Beaucaillou, St Julien

Planted on deep gravelly clay soils, this second-growth property is one of the most consistent producers in St Julien. Deep in color, with luscious blackberry fruit and classic cedary notes, this wine ages to give vibrant charm and balance.

Food pairings: Roast lamb or medium-rare beef
Vintage years: 2005, 2000, 1996

6 ❙❙   7 ❙❙❙❙❙ 8 ❙❙❙❙❙ 9 ❙❙❙ 10 ❙❙❙❙❙

11 Château Preuillac, Médoc

Huge investment at this formerly rundown château in the northern Médoc has brought great improvements in the gravelly vineyards and the winery. Now quality is on the rise, with soft, silky fruit and elegance showing in the wines.

Food pairings: Coq au vin
Vintage years: 2006, 2005, 2004

12 Château Potensac, Médoc

Situated in the northern Médoc with very old vines planted on a mix of gravel and alluvial clay. The wines are consistently good, with firm, ripe, black currant fruit and a full-bodied palate. They need at least five years to show their best.

Food pairings: Mushroom and eggplant lasagna
Vintage years: 2005, 2004, 2000

14 Château Belgrave, Haut-Médoc

This fifth-growth property on limestone gravel just outside the St Julien appellation shows results from big investments. Meticulous winemaking now produces deep plummy fruit with coffee bean complexity and a harmonious finish. Undervalued at present.

Food pairings: Boiled lamb cutlets
Vintage years: 2006, 2005, 2002

13 Château Cissac, Haut-Médoc

Concentrated, chewy wines at this 125-acre property in the north of the Haut-Médoc mature into the classic, tasty, plum and raspberry-loaded style of old-style Bordeaux with fine, creamy tannins. Affordable quality drinking.

Food pairings: Onion-braised short ribs
Vintage years: 2005, 2003, 1996

15 Château de Camensac, Haut-Médoc

New owners have taken on the 160 acres of densely planted gravelly slopes, and the wine quality is starting to shine. Great purity of style; ripe, dark red fruit flavors, and a firm, fresh finish.

Food pairings: Chunk of mature, hard cheese, such as cheddar
Vintage years: 2005, 2003, 2000

16 Château Haut-Marbuzet, St Estèphe

Intense, fleshy, powerful fruit in these wines from 125 acres of deep clay soil close to the Gironde. The 50 percent Merlot gives immediate cassis flavors, while Cabernet adds the power and structure of the region. Reliable and good value.

Food pairings: Roast prime rib of beef
Vintage years: 2005, 2000, 1999

17 Château La Louvière, Pessac-Léognan

Owned by André Lurton, who oversees some dynamic properties in the region, this is one of the stars of the Pessac-Léognan region. The wine is dense with blackberry, raisin, and toasty fruit, full-bodied on the palate with a minerally, supple finish.

Food pairings: Roast goose with rich red wine gravy
Vintage years: 2005, 2004, 1998

19 Château Clarke, Listrac-Médoc

This abandoned property was bought by the Rothschild family and received massive investment, but the wines have taken time to deliver their best. Consultant Michel Rolland has been called in and delicious richness and power is starting to appear.

Food pairings: Roast pheasant with red wine sauce
Vintage years: 2005, 2003, 2000

18 Château Sociando-Mallet, Haut Médoc

Occupying a gentle, gravel slope overlooking the Gironde, this property has been totally transformed in recent years and now ranks with some of the best. The wines have intense flavors of blackberry fruit with spicy, savory notes and are structured to last.

Food pairings: Roast pork with herb stuffing
Vintage years: 2005, 2001, 1999

20 Château Chasse-Spleen, Moulis

Consistent performance at this large property on a gravelly clay slope. The 73 percent Cabernet Sauvignon gives structured concentration, but there is elegance too, with deep, dark blackberry fruit. A second wine, L'Ermitage de Chasse Spleen, is lighter but still good.

Food pairings: Herb-stuffed lamb shoulder
Vintage years: 2005, 2003, 2001

16 ▮▮▮▮ 17 ▮▮ 18 ▮▮▮ 19 ▮▮▮ 20 ▮▮▮▮

Château Smith Haut Lafitte, Pessac-Lognan

St Emilion

On the Right Bank of the Dordogne, St Emilion and its surrounding vineyards rank as one of the world's most beautiful wine regions. This is the region of small châteaux, with over 1,000 properties on 13,300 acres, most with their proprietors in residence. The main grape varieties are Merlot and Cabernet Franc, with small amounts of Cabernet Sauvignon.

St Emilion's wines are classified into Premier Grand Cru Classé (PGCC), Grand Cru Classé (GCC), and Grand Cru (GC).

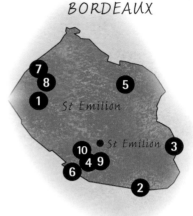

Ruins in a vineyard in picturesque St Emilion

1 Château Grand Barrail Lamarzelle Figeac, St Emilion Grand Cru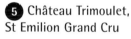

Now with Dourthe as long-term tenants, this property on the western part of the plateau, close to Château Figeac, is starting to show its true quality. With 75 percent Merlot and 25 percent Cabernet Franc, it has mellow, rounded blackberry fruit with firm, elegant structure.

Food pairings: Daube of beef
Vintage years: 2005, 2002, 2000

2 Château La Bonnelle, St Emilion Grand Cru

A delightful property on the edge of the appellation, where old vines and improved winemaking are showing in the wines. Merlot-dominated, it has soft, red fruit aromas with a balanced, elegant palate and light, structuring tannins.

Food pairings: Steak pizzaiola
Vintage years: 2006, 2005, 2000

4 Union de Producteurs de St Emilion, Aurélius, St Emilion Grand Cru

A Merlot-dominated wine from the excellent cooperative in St Emilion. Aging for 15 months in French oak gives a deep color and intense, ripe fruit flavors with lifted violet aromas and soft, rounded tannins.

Food pairings: Irish stew, with carrots, potatoes, and thyme
Vintage years: 2005, 2000

3 Château Lapelletrie, St Emilion Grand Cru

Exceptional value for money from this small property on limestone and clay soil in the northwest of the region. Thirty-year-old vines, 90 percent Merlot and 10 percent Cabernet Franc, give bright, firm, cherry and red fruit flavors with silky tannins and rounded oaky notes.

Food pairings: Grilled red meats, pasta marinara
Vintage years: 2005, 2002, 2000

5 Château Trimoulet, St Emilion Grand Cru

This family property, dating to 1713, occupies 42 acres on clay-limestone soil in the north of the region. A substantial proportion of Cabernet Franc and 5 percent Cabernet Sauvignon add structure to the Merlot, giving ripe, black currant fruit aromas with fleshy, silky tannins.

Food pairings: Moroccan lamb tagine
Vintage years: 2005, 2001, 2000

6 Château Teyssier, St Emilion Grand Cru

Great improvements in recent years at this eighteenth-century château following a change of ownership. Now 80 percent Merlot, and made in a newly equipped winery, the wine has ripe, red berry fruit, balanced by a fine structure and well-integrated tannins.

Food pairings: Beef tenderloin with mushrooms
Vintage years: 2005, 2000, 1999

7 Château Tour du Pas St Georges, St Georges-St Emilion

The surrounding area of Georges-St Emilion offers quality wine at affordable prices. Under the same ownership as top Château Belair, this wine is improving in style, with finesse, elegance, and silky, structuring tannins.

Food pairings: Baked pork chops with rosemary and oregano
Vintage years: 2003, 2001, 2000

9 Château Canon-la-Gaffelière, St Emilion Grand Cru Classé

This property has been climbing in quality for the last two decades, so now it ranks with some of the best. Forty percent old-vine Cabernet Franc in the blend adds freshness and spicy overtones to the wine. Sauvignon, and Malbec grapes give a rich, savory style, dense with fruit, herbs, and spice.

Food pairings: Herb-crusted spring lamb
Vintage years: 2002, 2000, 1998

8 Château Figeac, St Emilion Premier Grand Cru Classé

A high proportion of Cabernets Franc and Sauvignon at this property on gravelly soils on the St Emilion plateau. Raspberry-edged fruit and elegant structuring tannins make this one of this region's best—expensive, yet still undervalued.

Food pairings: Top-quality mature hard cheeses
Vintage years: 2000, 2002, 1995

10 Château Berliquet, St Emilion Grand Cru Classé

A prime south-facing vineyard site at this small property, with a new owner and winemaker restoring quality to its rightful position. Stylish elegance in the wines with crushed red berry fruit, integrated tannins, and a round, creamy balanced finish.

Food pairings: Slow-cooked lamb shanks
Vintage years: 2000, 1999, 1998

6 ▯▯▯   7 ▯▯   8 ▯▯▯▯▯   9 ▯▯▯▯   10 ▯▯▯

Vines growing, with the town of St Emilion in the background

Pomerol

This tiny appellation contains some of the world's most sought-after red wines. Adjacent to St Emilion, on a gently sloping plateau, its deep clay and gravel soil is ideally suited to the Merlot grape, which produces rich, deep-flavored, velvety wines at these small-scale, high-quality properties. Lalande-de-Pomerol is on the edge of the appellation on lighter gravelly soils.

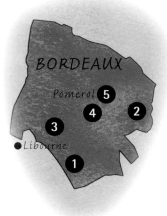

Dawn in Pomerol

1 Château Taillefer, Pomerol

This 30-acre property in the south of Pomerol has 75 percent Merlot and 25 percent Cabernet Franc planted on iron-rich sandy gravel soils. It produces pure-fruited wine, plummy and elegant, lighter than some but with style at an affordable price.

Food pairings: Beef Wellington
Vintage years: 2005, 2004, 2001

2 Château Le Bon Pasteur, Pomerol

Situated on the border with St Emilion, this 17-acre property is owned by wine consultant Michel Rolland. The wines, from 80 percent Merlot and 20 percent Cabernet Franc, are rich and intense with black currant and black cherry fruit, with a structured finish.

Food pairings: Pan-fried medallions of venison
Vintage years: 2005, 2003, 1999

4 Château Le Pin, Pomerol

This tiny 5-acre vineyard produces one of the most desirable and expensive wines in the world. The Merlot vines are meticulously cared for, and the wine is thick with fruit, layered, and complex, with elements of chocolate and minerals.

Food pairings: Rosemary-scented leg of lamb
Vintage years: 2005, 2001, 1999

3 Fugue de Nénin, Pomerol

Recently acquired by the Delon family, who also own Château Léoville Las Cases in the Médoc, Nénin's style is becoming more mellow and textured with lush, opulent fruit. This is the second wine, always a good buy at an improving property.

Food pairings: Roast chicken; semi-hard cheeses
Vintage years: 2005, 2004, 2003

5 Château La Fleur de Boüard, Lalande-de-Pomerol

Owned by Hubert de Boüard who also owns the excellent and expensive Château Angelus in St Emilion, this 48-acre property is undergoing a transformation. Impressive, scented wines, with deep, dark, spiced fruit and layers of complexity.

Food pairings: Roasted tender young lamb
Vintage years: 2005, 2003, 2001

Bordeaux Côtes &
between the rivers

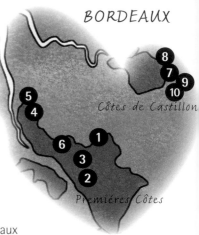

The fame of Bordeaux may rest on 100 superstars, but prosperity depends on the region's other 16,000 producers whose quality ranges from top-notch to average, good-drinking wine. On the Right Bank of the Gironde, the vineyards of Blaye, Bourg, Castillon, and Francs depend mostly on Merlot. Between the Dordogne and Garonne Rivers is Entre-Deux-Mers, which produces large volumes of red wine under the appellations of Bordeaux and Bordeaux Supérieur. Along the region's limestone south-facing slope, the Premières Côtes produces serious quality reds.

A vineyard in the Premières Côtes de Bordeaux

1 Château Bonnet, Bordeaux

Owned by André Lurton of Château Louvière fame, this large estate is on clay-limestone soil in the north of the Entre-Deux-Mers region. An equal Cabernet Sauvignon and Merlot blend, it has soft cherry and plum fruit with light, silky tannins.

Food pairings: Broiled steak and salad
Vintage years: 2006, 2005, 2004

2 Château Reynon, Côtes de Bordeaux Cadillac

Owned by Denis Dubourdieu, one of the world's leading oenology professors, this 93-acre estate is best known for its whites, but the Merlot-dominated reds are full of delicious black currant and raspberry fruit with a creamy texture and toasty oak.

Food pairings: Herb-roasted Cornish game hens
Vintage years: 2006, 2005, 2003

4 Château Falfas, Côtes de Bourg

A grand fourteenth-century estate with 50 acres, which have been farmed biodynamically for over 20 years. With 5 percent of Malbec (locally known as Cot) in the blend of Merlot and Cabernet Sauvignon, the wines have tremendous depth, chewy plummy fruit, and structured tannins.

Food pairings: Beef casserole with onions
Vintage years: 2005, 2003, 2000

3 L'Enclos du Château Lezongars, Côtes de Bordeaux Cadillac

This estate is rapidly improving as its British owners invest in the vineyards and the winery. The Merlot-Cabernet blend is from selected barrels and has sweet, elegant, ripe fruit with rounded fleshy texture and a touch of vanilla spice.

Food pairings: Wild mushroom tart with Parmesan
Vintage years: 2006, 2005, 2001

5 Château Roc de Cambes, Côtes de Bourg

Now a benchmark within the appellation, this 25-acre property, developed by Francois Mitjaville of Château Tertre-Rôteboeuf in St Emilion, uses low yields to give lush, concentrated raspberry and cassis fruit with spicy tobacco notes and a harmonious, balanced finish.

Food pairings: Broiled calves' liver with onions
Vintage years: 2005, 2003, 2000

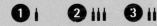

6 Château Pey La Tour, Bordeaux Supérieur

This property has seen dramatic improvements in the vineyard and winery in recent years. Now the wine has ripe, plummy Merlot fruit with succulent mid-palate concentration and a soft, rounded finish. Good value.

Food pairings: Braised beef in red wine
Vintage years: 2007, 2006, 2005

7 Château de Francs, Côtes de Bordeaux Francs

Part-owned by Hubert de Boüard of Château Angelus, this historic estate has 100 acres of vines on the clay limestone slopes of this tiny appellation. The wine has ripe cherry and plum fruit with streaks of minerals and light supple tannins.

Food pairings: Beef pot roast
Vintage years: 2006, 2005, 2004

8 Château Puygueraud, Côtes de Bordeaux Francs

A driving force within this region, Nicolas Thienpont uses top-class methods in his vineyards to restrict yield and develop ripeness. The result is a wine with deep plummy fruit, a sprinkling of herbs, and ripe, silky tannins.

Food pairings: Garlic marinated pork tenderloin
Vintage years: 2006, 2005, 2003

9 Château d'Aiguilhe, Côtes de Bordeaux Castillon

The old ruined castle, with attached vineyard and high-tech new winery, is owned by Stephan von Neipperg of Canon la Gaffelière in St Emilion. This is a gloriously deep wine, with dense black cherry fruit and increasing definition.

Food pairings: Roast duck breasts with cherry sauce
Vintage years: 2006, 2005, 2003

10 Domaine de l'A, Côtes de Bordeaux Castillon

Wine consultant Stéphane Derencourt farms this 10-acre property biodynamically, producing aromatic, finely textured wines, with intense blackberry fruit and velvety tannins from 60 percent Merlot, 25 percent Cabernet Franc, and 15 percent Cabernet Sauvignon.

Food pairings: Lamb osso buco with olives
Vintage years: 2006, 2005, 2001

Wine cellar in Bordeaux

Burgundy

The golden slope of Burgundy, known as the Côte d'Or, rises about 250 feet above the plain—a single sweep of vineyards on a long, east-facing escarpment, slightly tilted toward the south and capturing the sunlight in the folds of its hills. Made up of sedimentary deposits—mainly calcium-rich stone—the weathered slope offers a mix of soil types, from pure limestone rock to clay, shale, and soft brown loess. This patchwork of soils is the foundation of the quality classification that sees some grand cru wines grown just a few yards away from ordinary Burgundy.

Pinot Noir is the red grape variety here—lesser ones having been banned as long ago as the fourteenth century—producing the world's best expression of that grape—silky, sensuous, and seductive at its most perfect.

Over the centuries Burgundy has been divided and subdivided between families, so many vineyards have a multitude of owners, some with just a few rows in one appellation here and a few rows in another. Some market their own wine, while others sell to large *négociants*, who age, blend, and market the wine under their own name.

① Côte de Nuits

② Côte de Beaune

③ Côte Chalonnaise and
   Maconnais

④ Beaujolais

BURGUNDY

Burgundy experiences an
unpredictable climate, often
with hot summers and cold
winters, but with frequent
rainfall and sudden changes—
leading to significant
differences between vintages.

Côte de Nuits

Containing most of Burgundy's great grand cru vineyards, the Côte de Nuits is where Pinot Noir achieves its pinnacle of breathtaking complexity. From the less well-known villages of Fixin and Marsannay to the glorious depth of Gevrey-Chambertin and Nuits St Georges, the wines offer an expression of Pinot Noir that cannot be found elsewhere in the world. For this reason, the wines are extremely expensive.

Wine cellar in Nuits St Georges

1 Bouchard Père et Fils, Nuits St Georges

A long-established name, which is now regaining its reputation with exciting quality reds and whites. This has tight, concentrated cassis fruit, with minerally backbone and integrated tannins. Trade up to Les Cailles Domaine wine for more elegance and power.

Food pairings: Chicken braised in red wine
Vintage years: 2005, 2004

2 Nicolas Potel, Nuits St Georges

A quality négociant producing consistently fine wines across the range but particularly strong in Nuits St Georges. This wine is rich with dark fruits—blackberry, cherry, and plum, with herbal notes across the palate and finely balanced tannins.

Food pairings: Onion-braised short ribs
Vintage years: 2005, 2003, 2002

3 Louis Jadot Côte de Nuits-Villages Le Vaucrain

Quality across the range at Jadot, including this single-vineyard wine from the southern part of the Côte de Nuits. Ten-year-old vines produce deep-colored fruit, aromatic with ripe, red berry fruit and a concentrated, silky palate.

Food pairings: Wild mushroom risotto
Vintage years: 2006, 2005, 2003

4 Michel Gros, Bourgogne Hautes-Côtes de Nuits

There are several Gros producers in the Côte de Nuits, all good, but Michel has significant vineyard holdings in the good-value Hautes-Côtes. The wines are intense with black cherry fruit and are slightly earthy with firm, balanced tannins and a long finish.

Food pairings: Roast turkey with rosemary
Vintage years: 2005, 2003, 2002

5 Domaine de la Vougeraie, Pinot Noir Terres de Famille

The label says Bourgogne Pinot Noir, but most of the grapes have come from densely planted vineyards close to Vougeot. Vougeraie makes modern-style Burgundies, supple with elegant fruit, and a long finish with class well above its appellation.

Food pairings: Broiled lobster, with truffles or cheese
Vintage years: 2006, 2005, 2003

6 Bruno Clair, Marsannay Longeroies

Based at the northern end of the Côte de Nuits, Clair produces elegant, balanced wines. His Marsannay provides good-value drinking Burgundy with firm, structured fruit when young, opening out to vivacious red currant fruit and smooth tannins.

Food pairings: Roast loin of pork with red currant sauce
Vintage years: 2006, 2005, 2002

7 Domaine Ghislaine Barthod, Chambolle-Musigny 🛢

Increasing quality at this domaine has made it one of the best in the area. Poised, precise raspberry and perfumed rose aromas; a seamless palate of deep cherry with mineral depth; and silky, fine-grained tannins. A wine to age.

Food pairings: Seared lamb medallions
Vintage years: 2005, 2002, 2000

9 Domaine Rossignol-Trapet, Gevrey-Chambertin

Gevrey-Chambertin is the largest appellation in the Côte de Nuits. This domaine owns 35 acres along the slope, which are densely planted and worked biodynamically. The wines are harmonious, with fleshy plums and cherry fruit, and a touch of spice.

Food pairings: Roasted Cornish hens
Vintage years: 2006, 2005, 2003

8 Domaine Dujac, Morey-St Denis

Owner Jacques Seysses is based in Morey-St.-Denis and has built a fine reputation for his elegant, firm, structured wines. This has intense lively blackberry and plum fruit, with a touch of licorice and a long finish.

Food pairings: Grilled chicken with red wine sauce
Vintage years: 2005, 2003, 2002

10 Domaine Jean Grivot, Vosne-Romanée

Expensive but fabulous wines at this meticulous estate where quality starts with the health of the soil. Deep in color with perfumed, elegant aromas, rich-textured palate, spice-edged red berry fruit flavors, and silky, supple tannins.

Food pairings: Roast duck with pears and rosemary
Vintage years: 2006, 2005, 2002

6 🍶🍶🍶 7 🍶🍶 8 🍶🍶🍶🍶🍶 9 🍶🍶🍶🍶🍶 10 🍶🍶🍶

The Château of Gevrey–Chambertin, Côte de Nuits

Côte de Beaune

Centered in the ancient city of Beaune, the southern part of the Côte d'Or produces a range of red and white wines. Often softer in style than the Côte de Nuits, the flavors range from a chunky Pommard to the gentle perfume of Volnay and the rich fruit of Santenay, yet they still manage the complexity and age-worthiness of the Côte de Nuits.

A vineyard at Pernand-Vergelesses, Côte de Beaune

1 Joseph Drouhin, Côte de Beaune

Young vines from 1er Cru Clos des Mouches are sometimes declassified into this wine, giving it a richness of style. Classic open vat fermentation with punch down yields raspberry and red currant fruit with smooth, integrated tannins.

Food pairings: Cedar-planked sea bass with baby vegetables
Vintage years: 2007, 2006, 2005

2 Maison Champy, Côte de Beaune-Villages

Increasing quality at the oldest négociant house in Burgundy. Grapes come from the Champy vineyards in Pernand-Vergelesses and Saint Romain to give a light, clear style, with strawberry-edged fruit; soft, silky balance; and elegance on the finish.

Food pairings: Broiled salmon steaks with mushrooms
Vintage years: 2007, 2006, 2005

4 Jean-Jacques Girard, Savigny-lès-Beaune

Firm, structured wines from this estate. They need time to develop in the bottle, but then they become supple with bright cherry and strawberry fruit with well-balanced acidity, a dusting of spice, and firm tannins.

Food pairings: Assorted charcuterie of dried meats
Vintage years: 2006, 2003, 2002

3 Louis Jadot Côte de Beaune-Villages

Sourced mainly from vineyards in Chorey-les-Beaune and Ladoix, this is soft, juicy, accessible, affordable Burgundy, with smooth, supple cherry and plum fruit, a hint of smoke, and soft classic structure.

Food pairings: Mushroom- and marjoram-stuffed eggplant
Vintage years: 2007, 2006, 2005

5 Bichot, Domaine du Pavillon, Pommard, Clos des Ursulines

Quality is on the rise across the range at Bichot as new direction has upgraded vineyards and winemaking. When young, this Pommard is full of crunchy delicious fruit, which ages to silky elegance with a streak of earthy complexity.

Food pairings: Seared salmon with lentils
Vintage years: 2005, 2004, 1999

6 Domaine Tollot-Beaut, Chorey-lès-Beaune

Tollot-Beaut is a consistent, stylish producer with 60 acres of vines. This wine comes from the lower slopes just outside Beaune. It is a rich, spicy red, with dense cherry fruit, a streak of minerals, and a firm structure.

Food pairings: Seared carpaccio of beef with roasted baby beets
Vintage years: 2006, 2005, 2003

7 V. Girardin, Pommard 1er Cru, Grands Epenots

Better known for his whites, Girardin makes some excellent reds too, particularly this muscular Pommard. It gleams with sweet cassis and blackberry fruit, wrapped in firm, ripe, structuring tannins that need at least three years to harmonize.

Food pairings: Oven-roasted red meats or chicken
Vintage years: 2005, 2002, 2001

9 Domaine Bonneau du Martray, Corton

The most famous vineyard name in Burgundy from an outstanding grower. The reds come from the base of the Corton hill and are concentrated, tight, and structured when young, taking at least 10 years to open into perfumed complexity.

Food pairings: Roasted suckling pig or roast pork
Vintage years: 2001, 2000, 1998

8 Domaine Chandon de Briailles, Pernand-Vergelesses 1er Cru Ile de Vergelesses

From a stony vineyard the famous Corton-Charlemagne this wine captures the racy, slender style of Pernand-Vergelesses. It gathers weight as it ages, resulting in clear cherry and light plum fruit, stylish concentration, and a pure, balanced finish.

Food pairings: Rack of lamb, pink in the middle
Vintage years: 2006, 2005, 2002

10 Domaine des Comtes Lafon Volnay

An outstanding domaine, cultivated biodynamically, making expressive, silk-edged complex wines. This is a dense, creamy, black raspberry–fruited wine, with structured tannins, balanced acidity, and enough substance to last a decade or more.

Food pairings: Braised chicken Provençal
Vintage years: 2006, 2005, 2002

6 || 7 |||||| 8 ||||| 9 |||||| 10 |||||

A Comtes Lafon estate wine cellar, based in Mersault

Côte Chalonnaise & Mâconnais

The Côte Chalonnaise presents a different aspect of Burgundy. Quality is growing with individual producers and *négociants* investing in the region. Pinot Noir is the main variety here, grown in a number of named communes of Rully, Mercurey, and Givry. Farther south, the Mâconnais region is changing as the vineyards are replanted to Chardonnay, which is more suited to the chalky soil. Many good red Mâcon wines are made, but much of it is blended into anonymous Bourgogne Rouge.

BURGUNDY

Côte
Chalonnaise

Tournus

Mâconnais

Viticulture in Vergisson, Mâconnais

1 Domaine Michel Juillot, Mercurey 1er Cru, Les Champs Martins

Michel Juillot has a substantial spread of vineyards across the Côte Chalonnaise, but particularly in Mercurey. He makes deep-flavored, structured wines that mature to give firm, fruity elegance. Facing southeast, on clay limestone soil, Les Champs Martins is among his best.

Food pairings: Maple-glazed turkey with mushrooms and sage
Vintage years: 2007, 2005, 2003

2 Domaine H & P Jacqueson, Rully 1er Cru Les Cloux

The village of Rully is dominated by its splendid château. While its 750 acres of vineyards mainly produce wine for the large *négociants*, the quality at Jacqueson make this one to seek out for succulent, vibrant, perfumed fruit.

Food pairings: Roast pork with caramelized onions
Vintage years: 2006, 2005, 2004

4 Domaine Joblot Givry, Clos de la Servoisine

Old vines and low yields are the key to quality here at Givry's leading estate, where the wines are deep and concentrated. Clos de la Servoisine has a richness of style, oaky complexity, and the ability to age.

Food pairings: Slow-cooked lamb with lentils
Vintage years: 2006, 2005, 2003

3 Domaine Faiveley Mercurey La Framboisière

Large vineyard holdings and a fresh drive toward quality at this producer and *négociant*. Wholly owned by Faiveley, La Framboisière makes dense, firm wines, with cherry fruit, a streak of minerals, and earthy notes that round out over three to four years.

Food pairings: Roast cod with a tomato crust
Vintage years: 2007, 2005, 2003

5 Domaine de Villaine, Bourgogne Côte Chalonnaise La Digoine

Domaine de la Romanée-Conti. Certified organic cultivation, low yields, and meticulous winemaking make these exceptional wines. Deep, raspberry fruit, rich flavors, and harmony typify the style.

Food pairings: Roast pork loin with blackberry–sage sauce
Vintage years: 2007, 2006, 2003

Beaujolais

While Burgundy depends on Pinot Noir for its perfume, the large tract of land at its south—Beaujolais—relies on Gamay for its bright cherry fruit. Light, fresh, and juicy, Beaujolais has been renowned for decades for its Nouveau wines—to be enjoyed within a year of the harvest—but there is a more serious side to this productive region. Ten villages known as Crus are allowed to sell their wine under their own village name; each one has its own character and depth of flavor a world away from Nouveau. "Beaujolais Villages" is another expression of the region, a quality notch up from straight Beaujolais.

The Chiroubles wine region, Beaujolais

1 Louis Jadot Beaujolais Villages

From one of Burgundy's best-known *négociants*, this comes from the granitic soil that marks the best parts of the region. With good, bright, dark cherry fruit, this wine is sometimes sold under the Combe aux Jacques label.

Food pairings: Lightly spiced meatballs in tomato sauce
Vintage years: 2007, 2006, 2005

2 J. P. Brun Terres Dorées Beaujolais

Based in the unfashionable south of the region, Jean-Paul Brun uses traditional winemaking methods that build structure and depth of flavor into a simple Beaujolais. This has silky, plummy fruit and finesse above its humble appellation.

Food pairings: Chicken and vegetable casserole
Vintage years: 2008, 2007, 2006

4 Domaine Piron & Lafont Chénas Quartz

The grapes for this wine are grown on granite and quartz soils, hence the name. The vinification owes more to Burgundy than it does to traditional Beaujolais. A lovely, savory wine with great concentration.

Food pairings: Soft scrambled eggs with shavings of black truffle
Vintage years: 2007, 2006, 2005

3 Louis-Claude Desvignes, Morgon Javernières

Javernières is one of two named subzones in Morgon, and its soils, composed of decomposed schist and clay, produce wines famed for their structure and longevity. Louis-Claude Desvignes' version marries earthy fruit flavors to grippy tannins.

Food pairings: Prune-stuffed pork loin
Vintage years: 2007, 2006, 2005

5 Clos de la Roilette, Fleurie

Grown on clay-rich soils, the wines from this property have a floral character on the nose, tinged with ripe black currant and cherry fruit on the palate. They age gracefully, taking on Burgundian character as they mature.

Food pairings: Moroccan-spiced meat casseroles
Vintage years: 2007, 2006, 2005

Jura & Savoie

In the far eastern part of France, between the vineyards of Burgundy and the border with Switzerland, Jura and Savoie occupy a remote and beautiful part of the countryside. Scattered across the lower slopes of the western part of the Jura Mountains, the vineyards of Jura produce red wines from local grape varieties Poulsard and Trousseau, plus some Pinot Noir under the Côtes de Jura and Arbois designations. Farther south, with the Alps as a backdrop, Savoie produces red wine from the dark, tannic Mondeuse and small amounts of Pinot Noir. Few of these wines are exported.

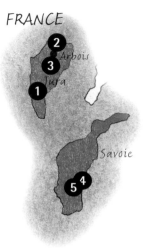

Cave de la Reine Jeanne in the Jura

❶ Domaine Ganevat Pinot Noir, Côtes du Jura

On limestone soil, in the far south of the Jura vineyards, Jean-François Ganevat's family estate is run along biodynamic lines. Aged in barriques (rare in the area), this wine is full of rich red fruit and well structured for aging.

Food pairings: Creamy chicken fricassée
Vintage years: 2006, 2005, 2004

❷ Domaine Puffeney Poulsard, Arbois (Jura)

Poulsard is a difficult red grape with a very pale color, restrained red fruit, and mineral nose, but it has a taut, robust, crunchy red currant palate with fine balance and it ages superbly. Puffeney is a legendary Arbois producer who ages his reds in foudres—large barrels, even larger than a barrique.

Food pairings: Trout with porcini mushrooms; spicy sausage
Vintage years: 2006, 2005, 2004

❹ Domaine de l'Idylle Mondeuse, Vin de Savoie

Brothers Philippe and François Tiollier run this 48-acre estate in the Combe de Savoie, halfway between Albertville and Chambéry. A Mondeuse made to drink young, this light red is easygoing, bright, and fruity.

Food pairings: Pasta with mushrooms
Vintage years: 2007, 2006, 2005

❸ Domaine André et Mireille Tissot, Trousseau Singulier Arbois (Jura)

This family estate is now cultivated biodynamically and yields are low. This wine is rustic on first approach, but it opens up to give gorgeous, dark, forest fruits with a lively palate, intense fruit, and ripe tannins.

Food pairings: Chicken in red wine
Vintage years: 2006, 2005, 2004

❺ Domaine Louis Magnin Arbin Mondeuse Vieilles Vignes, Vin de Savoie

From the best Savoie cru for Mondeuse, this wine includes fruit from vines more than 100 years old. The color is deep, with a spicy pepper and black cherry nose. The palate is surprisingly powerful. Will age.

Food pairings: Red meat pasta dishes
Vintage years: 2006, 2005, 2004

Rhône

There are two distinct personalities to the River Rhône. In the north it is a rushing, cutting river, forging its way between the rocky hillsides, overlooked by vineyards that cling to the slopes. In the south, it broadens outs, slows down, and meanders through the countryside, giving its name to a vast productive landscape. Both parts of the region, from Vienne in the north to the Rhône delta at Avignon and beyond, are red wine country, although there are some notable whites. Quality is moving up, particularly in the north, which has attracted a worldwide following for its dense, characterful wines.

The river has also given its name to a group of winegrowers around the world, particularly in California who love the style of Rhône wines and seek to emulate them in their own vineyards. They are known as Rhône Rangers.

Northern Rhône
2 Southern Rhône

RHONE

Much of the northern Rhône is swept by the dry, cool wind called the mistral, whereas the rugged mountain valleys of the southern Rhône offer protection from the wind, giving rise to many microclimates—each of which helps create a distinctive wine.

Northern Rhône

With steep hillsides, cold winters, and strong winds, the northern Rhône is a beautiful, inhospitable place. Vineyards cling to the slopes, often anchored by a single post, while vineyard workers pick by hand. Home to a single red grape variety, Syrah, the main vineyards are on the west bank of the river facing the sun—Côte Rôtie, St Joseph, and Cornas. Only at Hermitage do the vines cross the river, to take up a rocky, steep vineyard producing deep-flavored, elegant wines. Spreading out from the Hermitage hill, the wider area of Crozes-Hermitage provides a more affordable version of this wine.

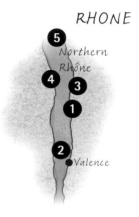

La Chapelle vineyard in Tain-l'Hermitage, Rhône

1 Domaine du Colombier, Hermitage

A small, family-owned domaine now moving up in quality. This has ripe, crushed blackberry fruit, overlaid with spice, chocolate, and savory notes, and bound together with powerful, structured tannins that take time to soften.

2 Jean-Luc Colombo Cornas Les Mejeans

Wine consultant, oenologist, producer, and *négociant*, Jean-Luc Colombo makes very serious wines, particularly in Cornas where he is based. This is solid with layers of plum, currants, and savory olive notes with herbs and structured tannins. A wine for the long haul.

Food pairings: Prime rib (rare)
Vintage years: 2006, 2001, 2000

3 Alain Graillot Crozes-Hermitage

In 1985 Alain Graillot abandoned corporate life and took up winemaking. Now with over 40 acres of Syrah, he makes fruit-forward accessible wines with supple tannins that will stand early drinking but still have the ability to age.

Food pairings: Roasted bacon-wrapped turkey
Vintage years: 2006, 2005, 2000

4 Cave Cooperative de Tain, St Joseph

Great value from this quality cooperative, which takes grapes from 52 growers in the region. This wine has blackberry and plum fruit, with toasty cocoa notes against an earthy, savory background. Tanins are firm, ripe, and structured.

Food pairings: Daube of beef with olives
Vintage years: 2006, 2005, 2004

5 Domaine Ogier Côte-Rôtie

This tiny estate used to sell all its grapes to Guigal, but now Stephane Ogier is in charge of winemaking and the style is rich, ripe with black cherries, black pepper, spices, and soft black fruits with structuring, silky tannins. Expensive and good.

Food pairings: Game or chicken casseroles
Vintage years: 2003, 2001, 1999

Food pairings: Baked duck breasts with green peppercorns
Vintage years: 2005, 2000, 1998

Southern Rhône

South of Montélimar to the Rhône delta the landscape softens to rolling hillsides baking in southern sunshine. This region produces 20 times more wine than the north with Grenache-dominated Côtes du Rhône as the main wine. Côtes du Rhône Villages comes from stonier soils, usually with a higher proportion of Syrah and Mourvèdre, while villages such as Vacqueyras, Lirac, and Gigondas have their own appellations and deeper, spicier flavors. Châteauneuf-du-Pape is on stony soil which absorbs the daytime heat and reflects it back to the vines, ensuring ripeness and bigger flavors.

The stony soils of Tain l'Hermitage, Côtes du Rhône

❶ Jaboulet Côtes du Rhône Parallèle 45 Rouge

One of the Rhône's flagship producers, Jaboulet's comprehensive range includes this good-value Côtes du Rhône from Grenache and Syrah. Peppery black raspberry and cassis fruit with a velvety texture and a long, balanced finish.

Food pairings: Mushroom and sage-flavored chicken
Vintage years: 2007, 2006, 2005

❷ Perrin Rouge, Côtes du Rhône Villages

Great value from the *négociant* arm of the Perrin family of Château de Beaucastel fame. The quality is consistent and well above many generic wines. Plush red fruits with hints of mocha and fig, with soft tannins and balanced acidity.

Food pairings: Charcuterie and Parmesan cheese
Vintage years: 2007, 2006, 2005

❹ Domaine de la Monardière, Vacqueyras Les Deux Monardes

Good depth and structure in wines from Christian Vache at this estate. Crushed plum and blackberry fruit on the nose lead into dark fig, licorice, and chocolate notes with a long, structured finish. The wine needs aeration before drinking.

Food pairings: Chicken chasseur with mashed potato
Vintage years: 2007, 2006, 2001

❸ Domaine de la Citadelle, Côtes du Luberon

This eastern outpost of the Rhône generally produces lightweight, easy wines, but Domaine de la Citadelle is run on serious lines with strict selection and low yields. The wine is thick with exuberant blackberry fruit and balanced with creamy tannins.

Food pairings: Vegetarian pasta dishes or red meat
Vintage years: 2006, 2005, 2003

❺ Domaine du Joncier, Le Classique Lirac

Not so well known as Châteauneuf-du-Pape across the river, Lirac has a similar style with less weight. This 75-acre organic estate makes chunky, blackberry-stuffed, herby, grippy wines that open out over time.

Food pairings: Veal sweetbreads with chorizo
Vintage years: 2007, 2006, 2005

6 Guigal Gigondas

Quality across a wide range of wines from this producer, although prices are high for the top wines. This Gigondas has warm raspberry-edged, figgy fruit with spiced chocolate notes and a fine, engaging perfume.

Food pairings: Braised beef with carrots
Vintage years: 2007, 2005, 2003

7 Domaine Jaume, Vinsobres Référence

Now with its own appellation, this former Côtes du Rhône Villages wine has moved up in concentration and depth of flavor. Pure plum and raspberry fruit with chocolate and toasty notes and a firm, balanced finish.

Food pairings: Mushrooms Provençale
Vintage years: 2006, 2005, 2004

9 Chapoutier Châteauneuf-du-Pape, La Bernardine Rouge

One of the most important négociants in the Rhône with extensive vineyards. Most of the wines are benchmarks of their appellation, including this peppered raspberry and licorice-filled wine with a fine-grained structure and long spice-filled finish.

Food pairings: Sautéed chicken with mushrooms
Vintage year: 2005

8 Domaine de Grand Tinel, Châteauneuf-du-Pape

Consistent, well-established property with 185 acres planted to old-vine Grenache, Syrah, Cinsault, and Mourvèdre, making structured, deep-flavored wines. Rounded, red plum and fruitcake aromas, backed by ripe, juicy, raisiny fruit and supple tannins.

Food pairings: Thyme-stuffed shoulder of lamb or cheese-based vegetarian dishes
Vintage years: 2004, 2003, 2001

10 Château de Beaucastel, Châteauneuf-du-Pape

One of the top producers in the Rhône, producing sensationally complex wines from all of CNDP's 13 permitted grape varieties. Deep raspberry and black fruits flavors with licorice and mocha lead into a tight, structured finish that needs time to soften.

Food pairings: Pork, sage, and mushroom casserole
Vintage years: 2007, 2005, 2001

6 ▯▯ 7 ▯▯ 8 ▯▯▯ 9 ▯▯▯▯▯ 10 ▯▯▯▯▯

The ruins of the fourteenth century château still remain at the heart of the
Châteauneuf-du-Pape region

Languedoc

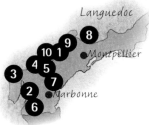

The Languedoc is an ancient and large wine-growing region, sweeping around the coast of the Mediterranean and soaked in sunshine. Rising just a few miles inland are a series of rocky hills, which are certainly breezy and sometimes even chilly. These changes in elevation and the shifts in soil type are being used to turn this bulk wine-producing region into a fascinating provider of quality wines from small individual domaines. With a whole range of grape varieties, including Syrah, Grenache, Mourvèdre, and Carignan, the flavors are big, ripe, and distinctive. This is the New World of France.

Grenache grapes soak up the heat in the Languedoc region

❶ La Sauvageonne, Les Ruffes, Coteaux du Languedoc

This occupies exposed, windy, rocky sites reaching 1,200 feet in the hilly Terrasses du Larzac in the eastern Languedoc. Eighty acres of vines, mainly Syrah and Grenache, produce powerful wines, pure-tasting with mineral complexity among the cherry and blackberry fruit.

Food pairings: Broiled steak with bell peppers
Vintage years: 2006, 2005, 2002

❷ Clos de l'Anhel, Les Dimanches, Corbières

A tiny property making top-class wines. Just 17 acres of terraced vineyards planted with old Carignan and Grenache produce a wine with dense, dark fruit and black peppery spice, which appreciates some bottle age to show its best.

Food pairings: Confit of duck with a spicy dipping sauce
Vintage years: 2005, 2001, 2000

❹ Château Sainte-Eulalie, La Cantilène, Minervois la Livinière

Top wine from young winemakers, Laurent and Isabel Coustal, who run this small domaine above the village of La Livinière. Syrah, Grenache, and old Carignan are blended to give concentrated blackberry and plum flavors with notes of herbs and peppercorns.

Food pairings: Roast squab with herbs and olives
Vintage years: 2006, 2005, 2003

❸ Château de Pennautier, Cabardès

Ripe fruit, with dusty tannins and complexity on the finish of this wine, which comes from a historic estate on the outskirts of Carcassonne. Winemaker Bertrand Seube, formerly of Mouton Rothschild, has moderated the oak influence to let the fruit shine.

Food pairings: Simple broiled steak and fried potatoes
Vintage years: 2007, 2006, 2003

❺ Clos Centeilles Capitelle, Minervois

Consistent quality from Daniel Domergue, who has revived the tradition of making great wines from Cinsault. Careful winemaking and a long *cuvaison* gives this wine spicy, structured fruit with elegance and a silky finish.

Food pairings: Herb-crusted rack of lamb
Vintage years: 2005, 2001, 2000

6 Château des Erles, Cuvée des Ardoises, Fitou

"Flying winemakers" Jacques and Francois Lurton make this fruit-forward blend of Syrah, Grenache, and Carignan at this estate on the rugged slopes between Fitou and Corbières. Trade up to the main wine, Château des Erles, when you find it.

Food pairings: Hearty, meaty hamburgers
Vintage years: 2005, 2004, 2002

7 Château Camplazens, Marselan, Vin de Pays de l'Aude

The first vintage of this Grenache and Cabernet Sauvignon–crossed grape variety was 2005. It is deep colored with plummy fruit, bell peppers, blueberries, and a streak of tar, backed by firm, ripe tannins. This is a premium estate in the Coteaux du Languedoc.

Food pairings: White bean and chorizo casserole
Vintage year: 2005

9 Mas de Daumas Gassac, Vin de Pays de l'Hérault

Aimé Guibert was the pioneer for quality in the Languedoc. His wines are all the better for the age and concentration of his vines. The red is fine-structured, dense, and powerful—mainly Cabernet Sauvignon with a handful of other varieties adding personality.

Food pairings: Chicken and mushroom casserole
Vintage years: 2004, 2001, 1998

8 Domaine l'Hortus, Grande Cuvée Pic-St-Loup

A leading estate in this distinctive hilly enclave within the Coteaux du Languedoc. Warm days and cool nights allow the Syrah, Grenache, and Mourvèdre grapes to ripen slowly, providing savory, spicy red fruit flavors with silky structured tannins.

Food pairings: Beef and olive ravioli
Vintage years: 2005, 2001, 2000

10 Laurent Miquel, Syrah Vin de Pays d'Oc

Based at Château Cazal Viel in St Chinian, Laurent Miquel has access to over 300 acres of mature, low-yielding vines, grown on a near-organic basis. This is a full-bodied, plummy spicy wine, with structuring, soft tannins.

Food pairings: Meaty pasta dishes or pizza
Vintage years: 2007, 2006, 2005

6 ▯▯ 7 ▯ 8 ▯▯▯ 9 ▯▯▯▯ 10 ▯

Fermenting red must is aerated by flowing into a tank

Roussillon

Half Catalan, half French, the region of Roussillon is tucked between the Languedoc and the Spanish border. Hot, dry, and swept almost continuously by winds from the north, Roussillon is a changing region. The old wines made by old-fashioned cooperatives are still there, but there is a new wave of producers—dynamic, questioning, and prepared to move up the hill to find the right terroir. But the best of the old remains with rich, complex wines such as Banyuls and Maury—deep concentrated expressions of old Grenache, fortified with alcohol, and aged for decades.

Bush vines is Roussillon

1 Mas Amiel Maury Cuvée Spéciale 15 Ans d'Age

Delicious Vin Doux Naturel from this historic property, mainly Grenache, aged in glass demijohns in the open sunshine. The result is an intense, caramel, rich non-vintage with coffee, almonds, and prunes coming through on the finish.

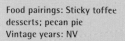

Food pairings: Sticky toffee desserts; pecan pie
Vintage years: NV

2 Domaine Gauby, Vieilles Vignes, Côtes du Roussillon Villages

Gérard Gauby is a man obsessed by quality, biodynamics, and the health of his vines. The intense, vibrant, layered spice and red fruit flavors in this blend of Grenache, Carignan, Syrah, and Mourvèdre are the result of that passion.

Food pairings: Slow-roasted pork with rosemary and garlic
Vintage years: 2004, 2003, 2000

4 Mas Blanc, La Coume, Banyuls

Grown on steep, terraced vineyards, within sight of the sea and close to the Spanish border, Banyuls is a rich, chocolaty, raisiny gem of a wine. It is a Vin Doux Naturel, fortified to 16.5 percent and aged in oak for 30 months.

Food pairings: Chocolate pot de crème or pour it over vanilla ice cream
Vintage years: 2003, 2001, 1998

3 Domaine du Clos des Fées, Les Sorcières, Côtes du Roussillon-Villages

Owned by former sommelier Hervé Bizeuil, who is discovering how much hard work goes into creating a wine. Old-vine Carignan and Grenache plus Syrah provide lively, concentrated red berry fruits with minerals and a dusting of spice.

Food pairings: Broiled lamb's liver with onions
Vintage years: 2007, 2006, 2005

5 Domaine de Casenove, La Garrigue, Côtes du Roussillon

Former photojournalist Etienne Montes has taken over the family property and focuses on quality with old vines, low yields, and a top-flight consultant. Carignan, Grenache, and Syrah provide dark, textured fruit with chocolate, cherry, and tobacco notes.

Food pairings: Grilled red meats or hamburgers
Vintage years: 2006, 2005, 2004

Provence

Best known for its light, fresh, and fruity rosé wine,
Provence is a beautiful, tourist hot spot, also home to
a number of good producers making notable reds from
blends of Syrah, Mourvèdre, Grenache, and Cabernet
Sauvignon. Many of these winemakers are newcomers
to the area, changing their lives and investing their
money in this sunny, breezy climate. The main appellation
is Côtes de Provence, which stretches across the eastern part
of the region, from the warmer coast to the cool hills. Altitude is
important to extend ripening to achieve better flavors. On the coast, the
high, terraced, rocky vineyards of Bandol provide some of the best reds.

The stunning Domaine Richeaume, Aix-en-Provence

1 Domaine de la Bégude, Bandol

Improving quality at this estate, recently acquired by the Tari family from Bordeaux. At 1,400 feet, overlooking the sea, 30-year-old Mourvèdre grapes with 10 percent Grenache provide sweet cherry and black currant fruit with a streak of herbal spiciness across the finish.

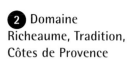

Food pairings: Beef tenderloin ragout with olives
Vintage years: 2003, 2000, 1999

2 Domaine Richeaume, Tradition, Côtes de Provence

Mainly reds at this organically minded estate, now run by California-trained Sylvain Hoesch, who has taken over from his father. Tradition is a rich, meaty wine, with roasted plum and berry flavors.

Food pairings: Roast pork with herb stuffing
Vintage years: 2006, 2005, 2004

4 Château Revelette, Le Grand Rouge, Coteaux d'Aix-en-Provence

Run by Peter Fischer, a California-trained winemaker, this 60-acre estate is one of the highest in the region at around 1,200 feet. A 50/50 blend of Syrah and Cabernet, Le Grand Rouge has plush black cherry and blueberry fruit with firm tannins.

Food pairings: Mushroom, eggplant, and tomato lasagna
Vintage years: 2005, 2004, 2001

3 Vignelaure Esprit de Nijinsky, Vin de Pays des Coteaux du Verdon

This famed estate is now back on track after a few changes in ownership. High-altitude vineyards are most suited to Cabernet Sauvignon and Syrah. Esprit is the good-value red with soft black fruit, dusty tannins, and spice.

Food pairings: Grilled chicken and salad
Vintage years: 2007, 2006, 2005

5 Domaines Ott, Château Romassan, Bandol

Robust savory, spicy, black currant and morello cherry flavours in this Mourvèdre, Cinsault, Grenache, and Syrah blend wine, grown on terraced vineyards at this historic property in the heart of the Bandol.

Food pairings: Five-spiced broiled chicken or pork
Vintage years: 2003, 2002, 2001

Southwest France

From the edge of Bordeaux to the border with Spain, and inland across to the vineyards of Tarn, the southwest corner of France contains a terrific diversity of wine regions. Some, like Bergerac, are hardly different in style from the more prestigious neighboring Bordeaux, while others such as Cahors and Madiran use local varieties, giving rugged, sometimes rustic flavors, always providing a taste of the terroir. Besides the many appellations of the region, there is a substantial production of Vin de Pays de Gascogne, much of it good-quality, easy-drinking wine made by well-organized cooperatives.

FRANCE

Southwest

Toulouse

A vineyard in Bergerac

1 Château le Roc, Cuvée Don Quichotte, Côtes du Frontonnais

This small appellation, just north of Toulouse, is home to the Nègrette grape, which produces soft, juicy, youthful wines with violet aromas and light spicy fruit. Don Quichotte has Syrah in the blend, giving deeper, spicier flavors.

Food pairings: Coarse-cut farmhouse pâté and crusty bread
Vintage years: 2007, 2006, 2005

2 Château Tour des Gendres, La Gloire de Mon Père, Bergerac

This 100-acre estate produces impressive wines from a blend of Merlot and Cabernet and Malbec grapes. This Cuvée has prolonged extraction and is inky and concentrated, with flavors of plum, cherry, and spice.

Food pairings: Duck with plum sauce
Vintage years: 2005, 2001, 2000

4 Château du Cèdre, Le Prestige, Cahors

Famous for centuries for the depth and color of its wines, Cahors is mainly planted with Malbec grape, locally known as "Cot." Château du Cèdre represents the new face of Cahors, making dark, richly textured, chocolaty wines.

Food pairings: Red meat pasta dishes such as lasagna
Vintage years: 2003, 2001, 2000

3 Château Lagrezette, Cahors

A recently revitalized 160-acre estate, now with Michel Rolland consulting, using top-quality, classic techniques to make firm, full-bodied wines, full of juicy plum and cassis flavors with chewy, structuring tannins.

Food pairings: Italian sausage and white bean stew
Vintage years: 2004, 2001, 2000

5 Château Montus, Madiran

Alain Brumont owns some of the best land in Madiran, planted to Tannat and Cabernet Sauvignon. The wines are deep, structured, and powerful with ripe plum, mocha, and chocolate-edged fruit and demand at least five years to achieve harmony.

Food pairings: Red meat casseroles
Vintage years: 2005, 2000, 1998

Loire

The Loire is the longest river in France, meandering from the center of France to meet the Atlantic at Nantes. Along its length are many wine regions providing dry whites, sweet whites, sparkling whites, rosés, and, increasingly, significant reds. Fragrant Pinot Noirs from Sancerre; crunchy, ageworthy Cabernet Franc–based Bourgueil and St Nicolas-de-Bourgueil; and silky, scented Chinon all provide distinctive, food-friendly drinking. Cabernet Franc also appears in Saumur and Saumur-Champigny, where its violets and raspberry fruit provide fresh, fruity reds that can mature into complex wines.

FRANCE

Wine cellar of Clos Rougeard, Saumur-Champigny

1 Yannick Amirault, Bourgueil Les Quartiers

Fifty acres of Cabernet Franc vines split between St-Nicholas-de-Bourgueil and Bourgueil are meticulously cared for. The wine is dark with deep raspberry and cassis fruit, a toasty, minerally edge, and tannins that need time to soften.

Food pairings: Roasted chicken with herbs and garlic
Vintage years: 2006, 2005, 2003

2 Clos Rougeard Saumur-Champigny

Top-class wines from the Foucault family, who have 25 acres of vines and make this intensely colored, cassis-shot wine, layered with chocolate, cloves, and white pepper, backed by fresh acidity, silky tannins, and a long balanced finish.

Food pairings: Wild mushroom risotto
Vintage years: 2006, 2005, 2003

3 Château du Hureau, Saumur-Champigny

Phillipe Vatan has run this 40-acre family estate for 20 years and has driven quality forward year by year. Old Cabernet Franc vines, planted on deep limestone tufa, produce soft, smoky red, raspberry-edged fruit, with light silky tannins.

Food pairings: Roast pork loin
Vintage years: 2006, 2005, 2003

4 Domaine Jean-Paul Balland Sancerre

Burgundy-trained daughter Isabelle has joined this family domaine, which produces mainly white Sancerres, as well as this Sancerre Rouge from Pinot Noir grapes grown on chalky clay soils. Charming red berry fruit with a palate of ripe raspberries and cool minerally flavors

Food pairings: Seared salmon fillet with fennel
Vintage years: 2006, 2005, 2002

5 Bernard Baudry Chinon

One of the new stars of Chinon, with 60 acres of Cabernet Franc. This domaine wine comes from alluvial gravel and hillside clay. It has a dark ruby color, with well-extracted currant and olive notes, good length, and gentle tannic balance.

Food pairings: Cumin-spiced butterflied lamb roast
Vintage years: 2005, 2004, 2001

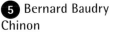

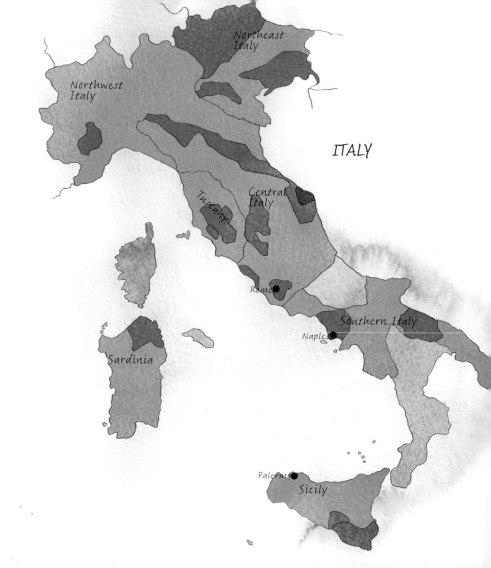

Northeast
Italy

Northwest
Italy

ITALY

Tuscany

Central
Italy

Rome

Southern Italy

Naples

Sardinia

Palermo

Sicily

Italy

With an ancient history of wine-making and a plethora of native grape varieties, Italy is one of the most exciting wine-producing countries in the world. It is also one of the largest, vying with France year after year for the most production.

Diversity in vineyard sites, and a patchwork of soils—including limestone, clay, slate, and volcanic basalt—allows Italian producers to create wines to suit all tastes and pockets. Italy's quality grading system awards wines from defined regions either DOC (Denominazione di Origine Controllata) or DOCG (Denominazione di Origine Controllata e Garantita) status. Revised and improved several times, the DOC system is not perfect, but it does provide a foundation for understanding Italian wines. The IGT (Indicazione Geografica Tipica) status, equivalent to France's Vins de Pays, is a useful designation for many quality producers who prefer to innovate outside the DOC regulations.

In recent years the wines of Piedmont, Veneto, and Tuscany have dominated Italian wine culture. Piedmont is famed for its tannic age-worthy Nebbiolo wines such as Barolo and Barbaresco. The Veneto offers lighter reds such as Valpolicella but also musters depth and power in Amarone della Valpolicella, made from semi-dried grapes. Tuscany is blessed with spectacular hills making equally spectacular wines, and quality is improving across the region. Chianti Classico, Brunello di Montalcino, and Vino Nobile di Montepulciano, mostly made from the same grape mix, all reflect a different aspect of the region.

The deep south of Italy and the islands of Sicily and Sardinia are acquiring a reputation for flavor and value for money as new technology moves into the wineries and new expertise consults in the vineyards.

Northwest Italy

Frequently shrouded in mist, the hills of Piedmont in
northwest Italy are home to some of the country's
most exciting, fundamentally flavorsome wines.
Nebbiolo, the king of grapes here, has gradually
softened in recent years thanks to moves to create
less austere styles, but it is still deep, sumptuous,
and complex. Barbaresco provides a more accessible
version of this grape, while Dolcetto and Barbera
provide affordable, characterful wines.

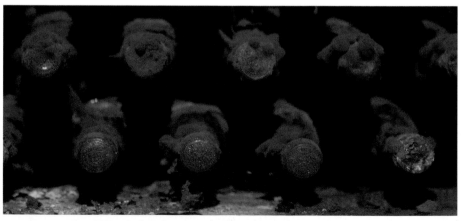

Barolo in the cellar of Angelo Gaja, Piedmont

1 G. D. Vajra, Barolo le Albe

Vajra's soft, supple Le Albe tends to be gentler than many Barolos, with the emphasis on elegant, soft, violet and raspberry-tinged fruit suitable for youthful drinking. Aged in large Slavonian oak rather than small barriques, the varietal flavors shine out with clear definition.

Food pairings: Calves' liver with onions
Vintage years: 2004, 2003, 2001

2 Elio Altare, Dolcetto d'Alba

Elio Altare has a fine reputation for his outstanding Barolos, but he also produces one of the best Dolcettos in the region, with dense ripe berry and plum fruit with hints of tobacco, flowers, and licorice in a light, juicy, structured wine.

Food pairings: Pasta al sugo (pasta with tomato sauce)
Vintage years: 2007, 2006, 2004

4 Giuseppe Mascarello, Nebbiolo Langhe

A good, well-priced introduction to quality Nebbiolo from leading Barolo producer Mascarello, whose Barolos are polished, expensive gems. Perfumed and elegant, this regional wine could easily be mistaken for a Barbaresco.

Food pairings: Antipasto prosciutto
Vintage years: 2006, 2004, 2001

3 Aldo Conterno, Nebbiolo Langhe Il Favot

Aldo Conterno is one of Piedmont's legendary producers and his Barolos fetch stellar prices. Il Favot, a more affordable version of Conterno's Barolos, is still incredibly complex with blackberry fruit, truffle, and savory notes.

Food pairings: Roast loin of pork
Vintage years: 2006, 2004, 2003

5 Fontanafredda, Barolo Serralunga d'Alba

This historic company produces a range from top-notch Barolo to Barbera and Dolcetto. Serralunga d'Alba is a classic Barolo terroir, renowned for its potent, long-lived wines. This particular example is expressive and rich, but it retains its core of steel.

Food pairings: Mushroom-stuffed veal
Vintage years: 2004, 2001, 2000

1 2 3 4 5

6 Vittorio Bera et Figli, Barbera d'Asti Ronco Malo

The Bera family vineyards are on steep, chalky slopes on the fringes of the Langhe hills. They are cultivated organically. Ronco Malo is a classic Barbera d'Asti, with plenty of raspy acidity, velvety texture, and juicy red fruit.

Food pairings: Grilled veal with pepperoncini
Vintage years: 2005, 2004, 2003

7 Parusso, Barbera d'Alba Ornati

High vineyard density and low yields are standard at Marco Parusso's 50 acres of vineyard close to Castiglione Falletto. The wines are good across the range, particularly this Barbera, which has dark, smoky aromas, overlaid with forest fruits, backed by supple tannins.

Food pairings: Gnocchi with tomatoes and basil
Vintage years: 2006, 2004, 2003

9 Roberto Voerzio, Dolcetto d'Alba Priavino

Low yields and the lavish use of new oak have turned Voerzio's Barolos into regional superstars. His Dolcetto, too, is more than a notch above standard, with plenty of sour cherry fruit to balance its exuberant tannins.

Food pairings: Mushroom and tomato-based pasta dishes
Vintage years: 2007, 2006, 2004

8 Braida, Barbera d'Asti Bricco dell'Uccellone

Braida's Bricco dell'Uccellone is a big, complex, fleshy, red-fruited Barbera made in a modern style by one of the big names of Asti. Unlike many Barberas, Bricco dell'Uccellone has the power and weight to last for many years.

Food pairings: Mushroom-stuffed ravioli
Vintage years: 2005, 2004, 2001

10 Ceretto, Barbaresco Bricco Asili

Bricco Asili is one of Barbaresco's top crus. Nebbiolo grapes planted on south-facing slopes produce violet and earthy aromas; ripe strawberry and mushroom fruit with soft, silky tannins; and enough intensity and structure to age.

Food pairings: Bollito misto with chicken and beef
Vintage years: 2004, 2001, 2000

6 ‖ 7 ‖ 8 ‖‖‖‖ 9 ‖ 10 ‖‖‖

Barbaresco vineyards, Piedmont

Northeast Italy

Culturally diverse and topographically varied, this area encompasses the mountains of the Alto Adige to the plains of the Veneto and the rolling hills of Friuli. Valpolicella is the most famous name, but it is Amarone, made from partially dried grapes, that really gives a stamp of quality to these wines. Friuli-Venezia Guilia is tucked away among the hills—a collection of small producers makes wines here that are distinguished both in style and price. Many have championed the use of obscure, local grapes such as Schiopettino and Refosco.

Rows of vines in Mezzolombardo, Trentino

1 Foradori, Teroldego Rotaliano, Trentino

Often dismissed as a mere blending grape, Teroldego vines grow on the Rotaliano plain in Alto Adige. Severe pruning yields a wine with dark, chocolaty blackberry fruit. Elisabetta Foradori makes some of the best, with robust complexity and clean acidity on the finish.

Food pairings: Pasta with four cheeses
Vintage years: 2006, 2005, 2004

2 Tommasso Bussola, Valpolicella Classico BG

One of the Veneto's dedicated young producers with a growing reputation, despite only a small production. His cherry-fruited, perfumed Valpolicella Classico is one of the best for affordable, enjoyable drinking. Trade up to his classic Amarone for full-bodied complex flavors.

Food pairings: Eggplant baked with tomatoes and Parmesan
Vintage years: 2006, 2005, 2004

4 Moschioni, Schiopettino, Colli Orientali del Friuli

A rare but expensive opportunity to taste a grape variety rescued from the brink of extinction. Schiopettino is aromatic with dark color and violet, raspberry, and pepper notes. It comes from leading producer Michele Moschioni, who grows other obscure varieties in these hills.

Food pairings: Parmesan cheese
Vintage years: 2004, 2001, 2000

3 Masi, Costasera, Amarone della Valpolicella

Vines on slopes facing Lake Garda benefit from reflected light to extend ripening time, then the grapes are dried a few months on bamboo racks before vinification in the traditional way. This wine is raisiny with cardamom, black truffle, and earthy complexity.

Food pairings: Grilled meats with mustard relish
Vintage years: 2004, 2003, 2001

5 Livio Felluga Sossò Riserva, Colli Orientali del Friuli

From one of the grand estates of Friuli, this blend of Refoso dal Peduncola Rosso with Merlot and Pignolo is aged 18 months in oak. It captures ripe raspberry fruit, with herbs and balsamic spicy notes, combined with a full-bodied palate and silky tannins.

Food pairings: Spring vegetable risotto
Vintage years: 2004, 2003, 2001

Central Italy

Vines grow across the central swath of Italy from
Bologna (the gastronomic capital of this food-friendly
nation) to the edge of the Mezzogiorno (the sun-
soaked south). Many of these wines do not rise to
the heights of the top wines of Tuscany or Piedmont,
but they provide warm, ripe, affordable flavors from
varieties such as Sangiovese with its cherry-loaded
fruit and the juicy, plummy Montepulciano (not to be
confused with the Tuscan region of Montepulciano).
International varieties such as Cabernet Sauvignon and
Merlot also make appearances in this central region.

Dolcetto grapes

1 Gianni Masciarelli, Marina Cvetic San Martino Rosso, Montepulciano d'Abruzzo

Gianni Masciarelli is one of the stars of the Abruzzo and his estate is a flag-bearer for the region. This cuvée, named after his wife, boasts brooding, truffle-laden, dark peppery fruit and copious ripe, silky tannins.

Food pairings: Zucchini and red pepper casserole; Italian meatballs
Vintage years: 2004, 2003, 2001

2 Nicodemi, Montepulciano d'Abruzzo Colline Teramane Neromoro

The top cuvee from organic vineyards covers 90 acres of the region, including new DOCG enclave Colline Teramane. Berry fruit follows through to a full-bodied palate with blackberry and chocolate character, leading to layers of complexity.

Food pairings: Tornedos rossini
Vintage years: 2004, 2003, 2001

4 Umani Ronchi, Cùmaro, Rosso Conero

Despite being one of the Marche's biggest producers, Umani Ronchi has high-quality standards across the range. Cùmaro combines voluptuous berry fruit with a touch of oak spice, fine-grained tannins, and a clean, minerally finish.

Food pairings: Mushroom-stuffed peppers
Vintage years: 2006, 2005, 2004

3 Fattoria Le Terrazze, Rosso Conero

Le Terrazze's top cuvée, Visions of J, is named after a Dylan song, but it comes with a steep price tag for a Rosso Conero. The basic cuvée is far more affordable, and shows more ripeness than most while still maintaining fresh acidity and crunchy tannins.

Food pairings: Pasta with pancetta and tomatoes
Vintage years: 2006, 2005, 2004

5 Santa Barbara, Il Maschio da Monte, Rosso Piceno

Santa Barbara's wines combine tradition with dynamic, modern winemaking. This blend of 95 percent Montepulciano and 5 percent Sangiovese shows plenty of meaty depth and firm tannins in its youth, but opens up to reveal a densely textured, potent wine.

Food pairings: Pasta with pork and tomato sauce
Vintage years: 2006, 2005, 2004

 1  2 3 4 5

6 La Stoppa, Macchiona, Emilia-Romagna

A blend of old and new at this restored 60-acre estate where modern stainless steel stands alongside traditional large Slavonian oak casks. Macchiona is a blend of Barbera and Bonarda, full of chocolate and cherry fruit with a savory, meaty character.

Food pairings: Rosemary-stuffed shoulder of lamb
Vintage years: 2003, 2001, 2000

7 Zerbina, Marzieno Ravenna Rosso IGT (Emilia-Romagna)

Dedicated work in the vineyards has taken the family's 100-acre estate to the peak of winemaking excellence. This wine, a blend of Sangiovese with Cabernet Sauvignon, Merlot, and Syrah, has dark, complex, powerful fruit with ripe, round tannins.

Food pairings: Broiled calves' liver
Vintage years: 2003, 2001, 2000

9 Falesco, Marciliano IGT, Lazio

Falesco, a large estate on the Lazio-Umbria border, is owned by two of Italy's oenological superstars, Renzo and Riccardo Cotarella. This is an intense, brooding Cabernet Sauvignon that will benefit from a few years in the bottle to tame its structured tannins.

Food pairings: Pork chops with mozzarella
Vintage years: 2005, 2004, 2001

8 Garofoli, Rosso Conero Vigna Piancarda

Made from 100 percent Montepulciano grapes grown on limestone-rich slopes in the foothills of Monte Conero. Aged for a year in traditional big oak casks, this is an easygoing wine with vibrant, herb-tinged cherry fruit.

Food pairings: Hearty pasta fagioli with tomatoes
Vintage years: 2004, 2003, 2001

10 Colpetrone, Montefalco Sagrantino, Umbria

Local grape variety Sagrantino is thick-skinned and packed with flavor and has the potential to age. Colpetrone has become a benchmark producer of this variety, producing wines with dense, herb-tinged black fruit and an impressive structure.

Food pairings: Beef with olives and mushrooms
Vintage years: 2004, 2003, 2001

6 ||| 7 |||| 8 | 9 || 10 |||

Harvest-time in Lazio

Tuscany

Tuscany has been the center for innovation for many years. It was the first region to step outside the tight legislation of DOC and sell its top wines as mere Vinos da Tavolas. Now quality across the board has improved, particularly in Chianti Classico where better clones and lower yields have returned the prestige to this wine. Sangiovese is the main grape variety, but contributions from Cabernet Sauvignon, Merlot, and Syrah add depth and character to many wines. Super-Tuscans still abound, setting the pace and price for the region.

Poppies growing in a vineyard near Greve, Chianti Classico, in high summer

1 Capezzana, Barco Reale

This delightful ancient estate has been leading the way in the small Carmignano area just northwest of Florence. The main wine has deep, structured flavors, but this younger version has juicy damson fruit with black pepper and light tannins.

Food pairings: Roasted herb-stuffed veal or beef
Vintage years: 2006, 2005, 2004

2 Antinori Badia Passignano, Chianti Classico Riserva

This historic, quality estate produces a fine range of wines. This Chianti Classico comes from a single estate and has ripe berry and earthy characters, full-bodied with chewy tannins and a long, precise finish.

Food pairings: Rack of lamb
Vintage years: 2006, 2004, 2003

4 Fontodi, Chianti Classico

Giovanni Manetti has been replanting his vines and restructuring his vineyards, which are situated in the perfect amphitheater of Panzano's Concha d'Oro. Now totally organic, the wines have deep morello fruit with structure, elegance, and length.

Food pairings: Veal cutlets with spinach
Vintage years: 2007, 2006, 2004

3 Felsina, Chianti Classico

Full-flavored, chunky wines made from organically cultivated vineyards at the edge of the Chianti Classico region. The basic Chianti Classico, made from 100 percent Sangiovese grapes, has earthy, truffly notes and a dense ripe structure. Move up to the single-vineyard Rancia for outstanding flavors.

Food pairings: Pasta dishes with beef
Vintage years: 2006, 2004, 2003

5 Isola e Olena, Cepparello IGT

This is 100 percent Sangiovese, from some of the best sites on Paulo de Marchi's estate. Outside the DOC regulations when first made, it still retains its IGT status. It has ripe, deep cherry and raspberry fruit, full structure, and excellent length.

Food pairings: Roasted herbed chicken
Vintage years: 2006, 2003, 2001

6 Poggio San Polo, Rosso di Montalcino

This estate is one of the region's rising stars. The Rosso comes from the same vines as the main Brunello wine; only the youngest and freshest barriques are selected to give a refreshing vibrant cherry-soaked wine with cedar and earthy notes.

Food pairings: Broiled duck breast
Vintage years: 2006, 2004, 2001

7 Il Poggione, Brunello di Montalcino

A large estate with 250 acres of vines. The Brunello comes from vines at least 20 years old, all hand-picked and aged 3 years in French oak. The result is a rounded warm-fruited wine that is intense, powerful, and savory with smooth tannins.

Food pairings: Truffle and mushroom crostini
Vintage years: 2003, 2001, 2000

9 Querciabella, Chianti Classico

Biodynamic viticulture on a breezy hillside produces depth and concentration in the grapes at Querciabella. The Chianti Classico has gorgeously scented fruit with red berry and chocolate character and soft, silky tannins.

Food pairings: Roast suckling pig; roast pork
Vintage years: 2006, 2004, 2001

8 Poliziano, Vino Nobile di Montepulciano

One of the top names in Montepulciano, making smooth, complex wines which age well. Made from a field selection of Sangiovese known as Prugnolo Gentile, with Colorino, Caniolo, and Merlot, then aged in French oak. Asinone is the Riserva wine.

Food pairings: Bell peppers stuffed with mushroom and lentils
Vintage years: 2004, 2003, 2001

10 Tenuta San Guido, Sassicaia, Bolgheri

Probably Italy's most famous wine, first released as a mere Vino da Tavola in 1968 to get around the DOC regulations that did not permit its Cabernet Sauvignon and Cabernet Franc grapes. Outstanding in quality, intense, and long-lived.

Food pairings: Veal scallops with mushrooms
Vintage years: 2006, 2003, 2001

Sangiovese grapes being pressed in an old-fashioned press. In a horizontal press, plates from either side of a closed cylinder are brought together to squeeze the grapes

Southern Italy & Islands

This is the powerhouse of Italy's wine production, but for decades quantity has triumphed over quality. All that is changing as new technology is introduced into wineries and quality is on the rise. Now the focus is on vineyards, taking them farther up the hills to seek out cooler sites and matching soil with variety to achieve the best flavors. Native grape varieties such as Primitivo, Nero d'Avola, and Carignano are widely planted and offer deep, robust, full-flavored wines from Campania, Puglia, Basilicata, and the islands of Sicily and Sardinia.

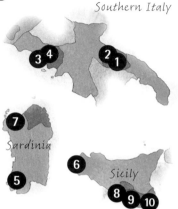

Vineyards in the Taurasi DOCG wine area, Avellino, Campania

① A Mano, Prima Mano, Puglia

A Mano makes a very good regular Primitivo at a very affordable price, but in exceptional years the top wine, a 100 percent Primitivo, is oak-aged and shows pure, direct blueberry and raspberry fruit with balance and complexity.

Food pairings: Broiled red meat
Vintage years: 2006, 2003, 2001

② Accademia dei Racemi/Felline, Primitivo di Manduria

Made by an affiliation of Puglian producers, working together to improve the image and quality of Puglia's native grapes, this 100 percent Primitivo wine, grown on terra rossa soil, is exemplary, with ripe plum and berry fruit.

Food pairings: Polenta with pork and tomato sauce
Vintage years: 2006, 2005, 2004

④ Mastroberardino, Radici, Taurasi, Campania

Radici, a 100 percent Aglianico wine, is the result of long research into the ideal *terroir* for this native grape. The chalky clay soils now regularly produce quality grapes that create a licorice- and berry-laden wine of depth and power.

Food pairings: Broiled lamb with roasted bell peppers
Vintage years: 2003, 1999, 1994

③ Feudi di San Gregorio, Serpico, Aglianico di Taurasi, Campania

Top consultant Riccardo Cotarella makes this wine from century-old pre-phylloxera Aglianico vines planted on the mineral-rich soils near Mount Vesuvius. It is dense, complex, and full of cherry, licorice, coffee, and sweet spice flavors.

Food pairings: Pheasant casserole
Vintage years: 2004, 2003, 2001

⑤ Cantina Santadi, Terre Brune, Carignano del Sulcis, Sardinia

From old vineyards in the Sulcis area of southwestern Sardinia, Carignano and just 5 percent of local variety Bovalledu produce this top wine from Sardinia's Santadi cooperative. It is full-bodied with complex blueberry fruit and sweet spice.

Food pairings: Roast lamb with rosemary
Vintage years: 2004, 2003, 2002

6 Donnafugata, Mille e Una Notte, DOC Contessa Entellina, Sicily

Nero d'Avola grapes, grown at altitude in the western part of the island, produce this top red. It is subtle, perfumed, and complex with notes of violets and incense melded to earthy fruit and fine-grained tannins.

Food pairings: Roasted chicken with wild mushrooms
Vintage years: 2005, 2004, 2002

7 Sella & Mosca, Tanca Farrà, Alghero, Sardinia

Tanca Farrà is the Sardinian dialect name for the area in which the Cannonau and Cabernet Sauvignon grapes that make up this cuvée are grown. The vineyard soils are iron-rich clays, which help give the wine its chunky body and structured tannins.

Food pairings: Stewed chicken with olives
Vintage years: 2004, 2003, 2002

9 Planeta, Santa Cecilia, IGT, Sicily

Now with four estates and over 800 acres of vineyards, the Planeta family continues to build on its success. One of its top reds, Santa Cecilia, made from Nero d'Avola is refined and elegant, with floral, plum fruit notes and light tannins.

Food pairings: Stewed octopus in tomatoes
Vintage years: 2006, 2005, 2004

8 Cos, Cerasualo di Vittoria, Sicily

Sicily's southeastern province of Ragusa is home to Cerasuolo di Vittoria, a recently granted DOCG for reds made from 60 percent Nero d'Avola and 40 percent Frappato. This version is light-colored and highly perfumed, with floral aromas lifting the berry and cherry fruit.

Food pairings: Onion and vegetable calzone
Vintage years: 2006, 2005, 2004

10 Tasca d'Almerita, Cygnus, IGT, Sicily

This large, aristocratic estate in the highlands of central Sicily makes some of the island's best wines. Cygnus is a blend of 60 percent fragrant Nero d'Avola, and 40 percent structured Cabernet Sauvignon with sour cherry and blackberry fruit, chewy tannins, and a balanced finish.

Food pairings: Sun-dried tomato and olive risotto
Vintage years: 2004, 2002, 2001

Vineyards at Giuseppe Tasca's top estate, Regaleali, Sicily

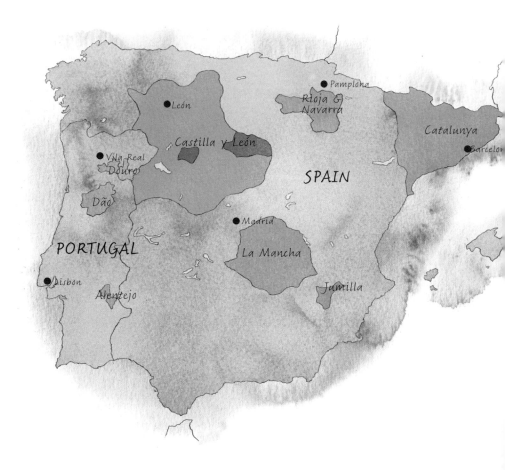

PORTUGAL

Lisbon

Vila-Real
Douro

Dão

Alentejo

SPAIN

León

Castilla y León

Madrid

La Mancha

Jumilla

Pamplona

Rioja &
Navarra

Catalunya

Barcelona

Spain & Portugal

Both Spain and Portugal have a long tradition of winemaking and now they are forging ahead with new investment in vineyards and wineries. Rioja remains Spain's largest and most famous fine-wine region, and its new styles are fresher, with more fruit and less obvious oak. Catalunya has become more serious about quality, especially the tiny region of Priorat, which now has one of the best reputations in Spain. In Castilla y León, the fashionable, high-altitude region of Ribera del Duero has expanded rapidly, producing deep-flavored, fine wines with prices to match, while emerging regions such as Toro and Cigales are learning to harness the strength of their grapes.

Portugal's treasure trove of local grape varieties is one of its greatest assets. Producers from Minho in the north to the Algarve in the south have realized the potential of their fantastic range of indigenous grape varieties. New attitudes, as well as new investments, are helping to create a world-class reputation for Portuguese wines. This is especially true in the Douro region, which is becoming as well-known for its dry reds as for its Ports.

Rioja & Navarra, Spain

These two regions are side by side in northeast Spain, yet they are dramatically different. Rioja's velvety flavors are created from Tempranillo and Graciano grapes grown in the chalky clay of Rioja Alta and Rioja Alavesa, while Cariñena and Garnacha grown in the warmer, lower-altitude Rioja Baja add color and aroma. French oak is replacing American at forward-looking bodegas. In Rioja's shadow, Navarra has struggled for recognition, but international grapes such as Cabernet Sauvignon and Merlot help bolster the flavors in this region's wines.

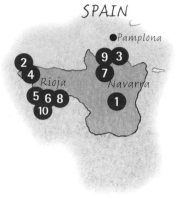

Wine-growing around Labastida, Rioja Alta, Spain

① Chivite Colección 125 Reserva, Navarra

One of the leading companies in Navarra with extensive vineyards. This wine is a highly elegant, oak-aged blend of Tempranillo, Cabernet, and Merlot with sweet-textured, lush fruit supported by firm, ripe tannins. Señorio de Arinzano is the single estate Pago wine.

Food pairings: Roast pork; roast suckling pig
Vintage years: 2004, 2003, 2001

② Finca Allende, Rioja

The new face of Rioja and a very stylish one. Based in Rioja Alta, this producer has a fine range, which, at the top-level Aurus, commands deep respect and high prices. This basic Tinto has ripe plum and cassis fruit, violets, warm, earthy notes, and fine-grained tannins.

Food pairings: Lamb chops with oregano and rosemary
Vintage years: 2006, 2005, 2004

④ Viña Ardanza Reserva Rioja, La Rioja Alta

Classic old-style Rioja from one of the region's best traditional companies. Aged for 36 months in American casks, this Tempranillo Garnacha blend is an elegant, complex, mature wine with dried berries, sweet spices, and savory, meaty notes with a silky finish.

Food pairings: Baked fish with herbs
Vintage years: 2001, 2000, 1999

③ Santa Cruz de Artazu, Artadi, Navarra

From Artadi investment in Navarra where old vineyards, an organic approach to viticulture, and modern winemaking produce this intense, 100 percent Garnacha wine. Fabulously complex, with vivid black cherry and forest fruit aromas, palate of silky red fruits, dried herbs, and fresh, structured finish.

Food pairings: Broiled meats
Vintage years: 2005, 2004, 2002

⑤ Marqués de Murrieta Ygay Reserva Rioja

A historic bodega with grapes from its own extensive vineyards; traditional winemaking with long wood aging. This wine is aromatic with savory mulberry fruit, smooth, firm tannins, and warm, spicy wood. Dalmau is the premium red made in a modern style.

Food pairings: Slow-cooked chicken
Vintage years: 2004, 2003, 2001

6 Telmo Rodríguez Lanzaga Rioja

Made by one of Spain's most celebrated winemakers, this is modern in style but full of regional typicity. Warm and generous with fresh, black fruit aromas; dense, herb-tinged, toasty fruit flavors; and a balanced, fat finish. Try Altos de Lanzaga for greater complexity at a price.

Food pairings: Charcoal-grilled zucchini and bell peppers
Vintage years: 2005, 2003, 2002

7 Muga Reserva Rioja

A traditional, family-owned bodega making excellent red wines. Mainly Tempranillo with Garnacha, Mazuelo, and Graciano, this is loaded with expressive, black cherry fruit, toasted coffee notes, creamy chocolate flavors with well-integrated tannins, and a fresh, floral finish.

Food pairings: Mushroom timbales
Vintage years: 2004, 2003, 2001

9 Roda 1 Reserva Rioja

A relatively new bodega with old, low-yielding vineyards. This is mainly Tempranillo with 14 percent Graciano and just a splash of Carignan and Mazuelo, aged in French oak for 16 months. The wine is lively and modern in style, full of ripe, spiced cherry fruit and elegant soft tannins.

Food pairings: Roast leg of lamb
Vintage years: 2004, 2003, 2002

8 Viña Herminia Crianza Rioja

A large company but quality is good, even at Crianza level. This is the modern face of Rioja with sweet black cherries, dried savory herbs, a sprinkle of spice and chocolate, with a fresh, balanced finish and just enough grip to combine well with food.

Food pairings: Red wine risotto
Vintage years: 2005, 2004, 2003

10 Artadi, Pagos Viejos Rioja Reserva

Great quality from this former cooperative, now emerging as one of the region's top producers. The 100 percent Tempranillo grapes grown at altitude on chalky Alavesa soils give perfumed, rich, dark cassis fruit with creamy oak, a hint of chocolate, and fine dry tannins on the finish.

Food pairings: Oven-baked lamb
Vintage years: 2006, 2005, 2002

Wine cellar of Bodega Muga, Haro, Rioja, Spain

Catalunya, Spain

Within this independent-minded region of Spain, Penedès was propelled to fame by the work of the Torres family, which has sought out grapes grown at different altitudes between the coast and 2,600 feet to create top-level, vibrant, distinguished wines. Even farther into the hills, in the tiny mountainous region of Priorat, the dry, mineral-rich soil produces some of Spain's most densely flavored and expensive wines. The surrounding area of Montsant—on flatter, more alluvial soils—is gaining in reputation.

The mountainous region of Priorat, Spain

1 Torres Salmos, Priorat

New in Torres range, planted a decade ago in the black "Licorella" soil of Priorat. Made from Garnacha, Syrah, Mazuelo, and Cabernet Sauvignon, aged nine months in French oak, this dense wine is full of juicy summer berries with sweet spices, licorice, and a smooth, toasty finish.

Food pairings: Lamb tagine
Vintage years: 2006, 2005, 2004

2 Alvaro Palacios Les Terrasses Priorat

Alvaro has created much of the excitement in Priorat. This finely crafted wine comes from the prestigious Gratallops subregion, where Garnacha and Cariñena combine to give powerful warm flavors of ripe blackberry, mulberry, and roasted plum with spice, oak, and silky tannins. Great potential.

Food pairings: Roast pork with prunes
Vintage years: 2005, 2004, 2002

4 Mas Collet Capçanes Montsant

Montsant doesn't match the massive style of Priorat wines, but has great concentration and character. Made from Garnacha, Tempranillo, Cariñena, and Cabernet, this has spicily sweet black currant and cherry fruit with smooth tannins topped off with vanilla oak.

Food pairings: Fava bean stew
Vintage years: 2005, 2004, 2003

3 Cims de Porrera Solanes Priorat

The "summit of Porrera," the vineyard is 1,500 feet above sea level. Old Cariñena grapes with Garnacha, Cabernet Sauvignon, and just a splash of Syrah give dark, sun-drenched, wild blackberry aromas with a deep spicy palate, herbs, and a minerally, oaky finish.

Food pairings: Pepper-crusted filet mignon
Vintage years: 2004, 2003, 2001

5 Torres Grans Muralles Conca de Barberá

Torres' top wines are gaining in style and complexity. Catalan grape varieties, including some rescued from the brink of extinction, combine to give broad-structured fruit, vibrant with raspberry and blackberry flavors, with herbal notes and sweet, elegant tannins.

Food pairings: Rack of lamb
Vintage years: 2004, 2001, 1999

Castilla y León, Spain

SPAIN

This splendid, castle-strewn heartland of Spain is home to one of Spain's up-and-coming wine regions, Ribera del Duero. Higher in altitude than Rioja, it has cooler nights, which help retain more acidity and finesse in the Tinto Fino (the local name for Tempranillo) grapes. To the west, Toro makes beefy, structured wines, also from Tempranillo (and called Tinto de Toro).

Vineyard near Penafiel, Ribera del Duero, Spain

1 Telmo Rodriguez Dehesa Gago, Toro

This traveling winemaker makes wine in Rioja, Rueda, and Ribera del Duero. Dehesa Gago is a great value, 100 percent Tinto de Toro wine, with thick, ripe, fruity, black cherry and blackberry jammy flavors, aromatic coffee, chocolate, and creamy oak.

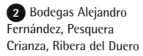

Food pairings: Spiced chicken
Vintage years: 2007, 2006, 2005

2 Bodegas Alejandro Fernández, Pesquera Crianza, Ribera del Duero

It was Alejandro Fernández who proved that Ribera del Duero was more than just a one-winery (Vega Sicilia) wonder. Now it is a major force in the region. Start with Crianza for complex cherry fruit, licorice, and spice, with refined, supple tannins.

Food pairings: Black bean and bell pepper salad
Vintage years: 2005, 2004, 2001

4 Pago de Carraovejas, Ribera del Duero

A top estate with 150 acres of vines on a windswept hillside. Mainly Tempranillo with Cabernet Sauvignon and Merlot in the blend, aged 12 months in French and American oak, this wine has deep cherry, tobacco, and mineral flavors with ripe, firm, structuring tannins.

Food pairings: Mushroom-stuffed beef
Vintage years: 2005, 2004, 2003

3 Aalto Ribera del Duero

The new project for Mariano Garcia, head winemaker at Vega Sicilia for 30 years. With organic vineyards (some owned, some leased), meticulous winemaking, and French oak casks, the wines are powerful, with a rich, meaty, cherry and chocolate palate and textured tannins.

Food pairings: Any oven-roasted red meat such as lamb
Vintage years: 2005, 2004, 2003

5 Dominio de Pingus, Flor de Pingus, Ribera del Duero

The second wine from this cult property. Made from 100 percent Tempranillo, which spends 14 months in new French oak. Deep purple, with sweet, pure, spicy aromas; chunky black raspberry and damson fruitiness; savory meatiness; and rounded tannins with a long, juicy finish.

Food pairings: Chorizo-stuffed pork
Vintage years: 2006, 2005, 2003

Other parts of Spain

The Spanish wine revolution continues in pockets around the country as investment flows in and regions define their styles and improve their quality. In central-southern Spain, the hot, dry region of Jumilla uses its local variety Monastrell (Mourvèdre) to produce increasingly well-made, sturdy wines. In the Northwest, Bierzo is becoming fashionable for its aromatic, fruity reds while Campo de Borja in the Northeast is realising the potential of its old Garnacha vines. Even in the plains of La Mancha there are fresh new vineyards and some top quality estates, helped by judicious irrigation and new technology.

Cabernet Sauvignon grapes on the vine

1 Juan Gil Monastrell, Jumilla

A rising star from Spain's lesser-known southern region, situated on poor stony soils on the highest part of Jumilla. Monastrell is the main grape variety here, giving black cherry fruit with layers of licorice, tobacco, and spice. Great value; sturdy stuff.

Food pairings: Mature cheddar cheese, served after dinner in place of dessert
Vintage years: 2006, 2005, 2004

2 Casa de la Ermita Crianza, Jumilla

A fresh approach at this forward-thinking, ecologically minded estate, mainly planted with old Monastrell vines, but with new plantings of Tempranillo, Cabernet Sauvignon, and others. This Crianza has generous plum and blackberry notes, with smooth, aged balsamic notes and a warm, spicy finish.

Food pairings: White fish cooked with tomatoes and basil
Vintage years: 2005, 2004, 2003

4 Borsao Tres Picos Garnacha, Campo de Borja

A group of three progressive cooperatives in the Campo de Borja, southeast of Rioja. Old Garnacha vines in high-altitude vineyards with hot days and cold nights produce bright, vivid, black cherry fruit, prunes, cocoa, and licorice.

Food pairings: Broiled red meats or tandoori-spiced lentils
Vintage years: 2006, 2005, 2004

3 Dominio de Valdepusa Cabernet Sauvignon, La Mancha

This historic family estate of Carlos Falco, Marqués de Griñón has its own single estate status (Pago). Meticulous viticulture, top-class winemaking, and a focus on international varieties makes it one of Spain's most outstanding estates. This Cabernet is full of intense, wild red fruits, spices, and chocolate.

Food pairings: Spanish lamb ragout
Vintage years: 2004, 2003, 2002

5 Martin Sarmiento, Bierzo

Made from the Mencía grape variety, typical of the Bierzo region in Spain and characterized by balanced, fruity red wines. Slate soils help add an elegant minerality to the palate, balanced by red cherry and red currant fruits and a hint of toasted oak spice.

Food pairings: Brown rice with pine nuts
Vintage years: 2006, 2005, 2004

  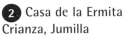

Douro, Portugal

This is one of the world's most beautiful wine regions, with terraced hillsides and deep ravines. Famous for their Ports, these steep vineyards are now becoming equally well-known for the quality of the dry red wines they produce.

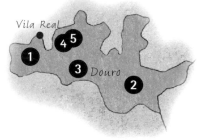

PORTUGAL

Vila Real

Douro

Tempranillo grapes

❶ Quinta do Crasto Reserva Old Vines, Douro

Perched on top of a hill overlooking the Douro, Quinta do Crasto makes wines from parcels of old, low-yielding vines made up of 30 different grape varieties. This is a complex, powerful wine with dark, perfumed, chocolaty fruit and a richly textured palate.

Food pairings. Bacon-wrapped chicken
Vintage years: 2005, 2004, 2003

❷ Quinta do Vale Meão Meandro, Douro

Legendary estate in high, hot Douro Superior, close to the border. The top wine, Quinta do Vale Meão, is outstanding, but Meandro, the second wine, is well worth its more modest price, with intense, juicy, plummy fruit; savory peppery notes, and medium-grained tannins.

Food pairings: Curry-spiced lentil and vegetable casserole
Vintage years: 2005, 2004, 2003

❹ Prats and Symington Chryseia, Douro 🛢

Joint project of the Symington family, who own the Douro's leading Port houses, and winemaker Bruno Prats. Made with Touriga Nacional and Touriga Franca grapes from top sites, this wine has intense, deep color; aromas of chocolate-dipped raspberries; and spice-edged, structured palate.

Food pairings: Roasted lamb
Vintage years: 2005, 2004, 2003

❸ Niepoort Redoma, Douro

Dirk Niepoort is one of the most dynamic producers here. Redoma is made from Touriga Franca, Tinta Roriz, and other grapes from high, north-facing vineyards. The wine is dark, full of raspberry and black cherry fruit, earthy and spicy notes, and a defined tannic structure.

Food pairings: Pork fillet, spiced with chile
Vintage years: 2006, 2005, 2001

❺ Symington Altano, Douro

A terrific entry-level Douro wine from the Symington family who take grapes from three of their estates in the Vilarica Valley, which are in the process of converting to organic. Ripe, soft, juicy raspberry and blueberry fruit with chocolate and spice on the finish.

Food pairings: Monkfish with red bell peppers
Vintage years: 2007, 2006, 2005

Other wines from Portugal

PORTUGAL

Recent investment in vineyards and wineries across Portugal is yielding excellent results. The sheltered, granite hillsides of the Dão region produce mainly red wines from Touriga Nacional and other local grapes. Farther south, on the wide, dry plains of the Alentejo new plantings are producing a wide range of quality wines from local and international varieties. Even coastal Estremadura, with its warm, damp climate can produce good quality wines if the right grapes are planted and yields cut back.

Vineyards near Chanceleiros, Alto Douro, Portugal

1 Quinta de Chocapalha, Estremadura

A small estate, fast gaining a reputation. Family property of Sandra Tavares da Silva, who also makes wine at Quinta do Vale Dona Maria in the Douro. Tinta Roriz and Touriga Nacional give rich, solid fruit with chocolate and raspberry notes and firm, structuring tannins.

Food pairings: Chorizo and tomato soup
Vintage years: 2005, 2004, 2003

2 Quinta dos Roques Reserva, Dão

One of the leading properties in Dão. Makes modern, approachable wines from Portuguese grape varieties. An old, mixed vineyard of Touriga Nacional and Tinto Roriz provides grapes for this wine, which has deep plum and blackberry fruit with spice and smoky notes.

Food pairings: Portuguese piri piri chicken
Vintage years: 2004, 2003, 2000

4 Luis Pato, Vinha Velhas Tinto Beiras

Pioneering winemaker Luis Pato now uses the regional Beiras designation instead of Bairrada, which gives him flexibility in his winemaking. But the wines are good. This wine is dark and intense with raspberry, cherries, prunes, coffee, and a finish of wild herbs.

Food pairings: Paprika pork with rice
Vintage years: 2005, 2004, 2003

3 Esporão Reserva Tinto, Alentejo

A large, well-run estate, with Australian David Baverstock producing quality wines across the range. This wine, made from Aragonês, Cabernet Sauvignon, and Trincadeira, is dense, ripe, and thick with savory fruit. Try Alicante Bouschet for vibrant, juicy, violet and spiced berry fruit.

Food pairings: Spiced duck breast
Vintage years: 2006, 2005, 2004

5 João Portugal Ramos, Vila Santa Alentejo

One of Portugal's top winemakers produces modern, fruit-soaked wines, many of them varietally labeled. This creamy, fresh raspberry and cinnamon-style Vila Santa is a blend of Aragonês, Trincadeira, and Cabernet Sauvignon, part foot-trodden, and aged in French and American oak.

Food pairings: Broiled red meats
Vintage years: 2007, 2006, 2005

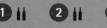

Port

Rich in deep fruity flavors, fortified and aged for many years in cask and bottle, Port is the traditional end to a grand dinner. Enjoy the nuts and figgy fruit of cask-aged Tawnies and Colheitas or lively, peppery, ruby, elegant Late Bottled Vintage wines; or experience the exquisite complexity of Single Quinta and Vintage Ports.

Port wine barrels of Taylor's Port, Vila Nova de Gaia, Portugal

1 Graham Vintage Port

Part of the Symington group, together with Warre and Dow, Graham's Vintage Port is a classic Port—rich, sweet, and dense with flavor, and capable for living for decades. Other fine vintages are 2000 and 2003.

Food pairings: After dinner dishes with chocolate or cheese
Vintage years: 1997, 1991, 1985

2 Noval 10 Year Tawny Port

This historic Port house has seen huge investment at its Douro estate. With extensive replanting in the vineyards, and a new cellar and warehouse, Noval has increased in quality and substance. The 10 Year Tawny is full of toffee, nutty flavors, creamy and long.

Food pairings: Pecan pie
Vintage years: NV

4 Quinta do Vesuvio

A grand historic estate in the Upper Douro where all the Port is foot-trodden in large, old granite lagares. A classic year was 2001. This wine is still dark and inky, dense and minerally, with a long life ahead of it.

Food pairings: Creamy blue cheese, such as Stilton or any hard cheeses, served after dinner
Vintage years: 2001, 2000, 1997

3 Taylor's Quinta de Vargellas

Elegance shines out of the whole range of Taylor's Ports, particularly their finely structured and perfumed Vintage. But the single-estate Quinta de Vargellas, made in years when a vintage is not declared, is a concentrated, composed, silky wine.

Food pairings: Any dark chocolate-based dessert such as chocolate mousse
Vintage years: 2001, 1998, 1996 1991

5 Niepoort Colheita Port

There are exceptional Ports from this small family-run producer. Colheita, a cask-aged single-vintage Port is a particular specialty here. Aged in small oak casks for at least seven years, it has floral, nutty notes; is smooth on the palate; and gives a fine, long finish.

Food pairings: Chocolate-covered figs
Vintage years: 1997, 1995, 1991

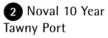

SLOVENIA
● Ljubljana

HUNGARY
● Budapest

ROMANIA
● Bucharest

BULGARIA
● Sofia

Eastern Europe

The winemakers of the former Eastern Bloc have had a challenging time in recent history. Communist rule encouraged quantity over quality, and when the pipeline to the Soviet market was suddenly switched off, many of the cooperative wineries found themselves looking for new markets. Vineyards have had to discover the needs of their new customers and rediscover the potential of their own lands and wine styles. International investment is starting to develop confidence, quality, and reliability in these regions.

Bulgaria is known for its reds, with Cabernet Sauvignon leading the way, although Merlot and local varieties such as Mavrud and Melnik add character to the range. The majority of Bulgaria's deep-flavored red wines grow on the sheltered, south-facing slopes on the south side of the Balkans.

Romania produces three times more wine than Bulgaria, but very little is exported. Cabernet Sauvignon, Merlot, and some light clones of Pinot Noir provide much of the red wine, but local varieties make rich, well-structured reds. The warm, south-facing slopes of Dealul Mare are noted for their quality.

There is substantial progress in the quality of red wine in Hungary, particularly in the south, close to the Croatian border. The loam and limestone soil of Villány produces soft, juicy Cabernets and rounded Pinots, while closer to the Danube, Szekszárd is famous for its Kékfrankos blends, locally known as Bikavér.

Slovenia has always been the most European of the Balkan states, in particular on its western border with Italy. Here, established families are once again able to invest and create quality wines from local and international grapes.

Eastern Europe

From the Adriatic coastline at the Italian border, spreading 700 miles eastward to the edge of the Black Sea, Slovenia, Croatia, Hungary, Romania, and Bulgaria have been producing wine for thousands of years. The climate varies across the landmass—maritime in the west close to the Mediterranean but dramatically continental across most of the area, with very cold winters and hot summers. The Black Sea has a slightly moderating effect in the far east of the region. This climate means that grape varieties and vineyard sites must be chosen with care to give each grape variety time to ripen completely.

Old-style transport in Svishtov, Bulgaria

1 Cherry Tree Hill Merlot, Dealul Mare, Romania

Dealul Mare ("big hill") occupies south-facing slopes of the foothills of the Carpathians, north of Romania's capital, Bucharest. This Merlot has soft, velvety fruit, with clear red berry flavors, light, ripe tannins, and a balanced finish.

Food pairings: Hearty soups; calves' liver in red wine
Vintage years: 2006, 2005, 2003

2 Prahova Valley, Cabernet Sauvignon Dealul Mare, Romania

There is increasing quality from the Dealul Mare region of the south-facing slopes of the Carpathian Mountains, especially in this Cabernet, which has ripe, rounded black currant fruit with a touch of tobacco and a soft, supple finish.

Food pairings: Bacon and mushroom-stuffed beef; sausage casserole
Vintage years: 2003 2002, 2000

4 Terra Tangra Cabernet Sauvignon, South Sakar, Southern Region, Bulgaria

Situated on the southwest slopes of the Sakar Mountain in the Thracian lowlands, this winery produces elegant, rounded wines. The Cabernet, with its attractive black cherry and bramble fruit, is rounded and complex with soft young tannins.

Food pairings: Lamb moussaka
Vintage years: 2006, 2005, 2004

3 Bessa Valley, Enira, Pazardjik Region, Bulgaria

Stephan de Neipperg, of St Emilion's Canon La Gaffelière, is an investor in this property 135 miles southeast of Sofia in the Pazardjik region. The wines show the true potential of Bulgaria. This Merlot-Cabernet blend is full of forest fruits, harmony, and balance.

Food pairings: Broiled beef
Vintage years: 2006 2005, 2004

5 Damianitza No Man's Land, Southwestern Region, Bulgaria

Grown on a five-mile-wide strip of land that once separated Bulgaria from its neighbors, this wine is made from Cabernet Sauvignon and Merlot. It is succulent, juicy, and full of red berry fruits and silky tannins.

Food pairings: Beef casserole, aged cheddar cheese
Vintage years: 2004, 2003, 2002

6 Byzantium Rosso di Valachia, Dealul Mare, Romania

Made from a blend of local grape Feteasca Neagra with Pinot Noir and Merlot, aged in oak for 18 months, this wine is full-bodied, balanced, and harmonious, with a dark purple color, spiced red-berried fruits, a touch of tobacco, and a soft finish.

Food pairings: Coq au vin, lamb kabobs
Vintage years: 2006, 2005, 2002

7 Movia Veliko Rosso Brda, Slovenia

Straddling the border between Slovenia and Italy, this 38-acre family-owned property is moving from organic to biodynamic cultivation. The wines are typical of the Collio region, including this savory, cherry and forest-fruity blend of Cabernet, Merlot, and Pinot Noir.

Food pairings: Roast chicken with herbs
Vintage years: 2004, 2002, 2000

9 Takler Heritage Cuvée, Szekszárd, Hungary

Ferenc Takler makes full-bodied, velvety reds at his small estate located on the deep loess soil of Szekszárd. This is a Bikavér, a blend of local grape Kékfrankos with Merlot, Cabernet Sauvignon, Cabernet Franc, and Kadarka, capturing ripe cherry fruit, tobacco, and pepper notes.

Food pairings: Meatloaf; broiled spareribs
Vintage years: 2006, 2004, 2003

8 Batic Cabernet Franc, Reserva, Vipava Valley, Slovenia

Located in the extreme west of Slovenia, Vipava Valley is swept by a strong wind that keeps diseases at bay. Batic, an organic estate, produces this elegant, rounded wine, with clear red berry fruit, chocolate, and a touch of spice.

Food pairings: Roast pork; broiled sausages with cabbage
Vintage years: 2006, 2005, 2004

10 Vylyan Pinot Noir, Villány, Hungary

Based in the extreme south of Hungary, close to the Croatian border, where summers are long, warm, and sunny, this premium producer makes a complex, herb-scented, cherry fruity Pinot with savory length and a creamy texture.

Food pairings: Tuna Provençale; roasted Mediterranean vegetable lasagne
Vintage years: 2005, 2004, 2003

6 7 8 9 10

A wine cellar in Maribor, Slovenia

Eastern Mediterranean

The southeastern corner of Europe is the cradle of viticulture. Vines have grown wild in this area for thousands of years, and probably for millions of years. The first wine was likely made by accident—delicious berries naturally fermenting to produce a mildly alcoholic drink. As knowledge increased, it is quite likely that the vines were cultivated, bringing together a number of vines into one area. It is also likely that the need to plant a vineyard and wait a year for the crop could have transformed the way of life for developing man as he changed from a nomadic creature to one who remained in one place, farming the land.

In Greece, the history of winemaking can be traced back over 4,000 years and wine trading back more than 3,000 years. Wines were transported in terracotta amphorae, sealed with wax, and usually marked with the name of the region the wine came from, making them the first wines to carry some kind of appellation, or designation according to provenance. The Ancient Egyptians also enjoyed their wines and even placed wine jars in the pyramids to accompany the pharaoh on his last journey.

The Eastern Mediterranean is still a treasure trove of native grape varieties, many of them grown in tiny quantities in local areas, and Greece is fortunate to have retained many of them. Sadly other countries, such as Lebanon and Israel, have abandoned or replaced their native vines with international grapes, in many cases as a way to gain access to international trade.

Greece

There is a refreshing new wave of enthusiasm and expertise in the vineyards of Greece. A new generation of winemakers, fresh from wine universities around the world, are looking at their vineyards and varieties to find the best for each site. Local varieties such as the soft fruity Agiorgitiko, which grows mainly in the Peloponnese area, and the structured, tannic Xinomavro from the Macedonia area of northern Greece are the key reds. Mavrodaphne continues to be grown for fortified dessert wines. International varieties such as Merlot, Syrah, and Cabernet Sauvignon are often blended in to soften the character of the local grapes.

GREECE

Wine-growing near Patras, Peloponnes—temperatures are hot, so higher altitudes are sought to grow the grapes

1 Tsantali Rapsani, Thessaly

A large producer with vineyards scattered across the country making wines at all price levels. This blend of Xinomavro, Krassato, and Stavroto is from the slopes of Mount Olympus in Thessaly. It is a supple, dark-fruited wine with touches of licorice and spice.

Food pairings: Mushroom- and rice-stuffed grape leaves
Vintage years: 2005, 2003, 2002

2 Mercouri Estate Red, Peloponnese

Located in the western Peloponnese, this long-established estate is planted with Refosco and Mavrodaphne, which produces a dense purple wine with tobacco and plums notes on the nose and soft, juicy cherry fruit and herbs on the palate.

Food pairings: Baked lamb with oregano
Vintage years: 2005, 2004, 2003

3 Papantonis Agiorgitiko Medan Agan, Peloponnese

Agiorgitiko is the main red wine focus at this family estate in the highlands of Malandreni. Medan Agan means "nothing in excess," and the wine reflects this balance with ripe cherry and plum aromas, minerally notes, and a touch of spice.

Food pairings: Stuffed eggplant
Vintage years: 2005, 2004, 2001

4 Gaia Notios Agiorgitiko, Nemea Peloponnese

With two estates, one on the island of Santorini and this one on the deep red soil of Nemea, this is one of the best producers in Greece. Agiorgitiko is Nemea's indigenous grape variety, producing intense, spiced cherry fruit wines with a touch of minerals on the finish.

Food pairings: Moussaka
Vintage years: 2007, 2006, 2005

5 Avantis Syrah, Peloponnese

There's new investment and enthusiasm at this well-established winery in southern Evia, where vineyards have been replanted with Rhône varieties. The Syrah has smoky bramble berries on the nose, with juicy spiced berries on the palate, chocolate and pepper notes, and smooth tannins.

Food pairings: Sliced beef in mushroom sauce
Vintage years: 2006, 2004, 2002

6 Pavlou Estate Xinomavro, Macedonia

With a new winery and old vines in the hills of the Amyndeon region of Macedonia, this 20-acre estate is in the process of becoming organic. Made from Xinomavro grapes, this wine has a deep color with dark cherry aromas and a smooth palate.

Food pairings: Pork with chestnuts
Vintage years: 2006, 2005, 2004

7 Gerovassiliou Avaton, Macedonia

Two miles from the sea in Epanomi, southwest of Thessaloniki, Bordeaux-trained Evángelos Gerovassiliou cultivates 112 acres of vines. This is an oak-aged blend of indigenous varieties Limnio, Mavroudi, and Mavrotragano, with dark berry fruit, savory, earthy notes, and a spicy structured finish.

Food pairings: Chile chicken kabobs
Vintage years: 2004, 2003, 2001

9 Alpha Estate 2004, Alpha One Red, Amyndeo, Macedonia

A new estate vineyard at a cool 1,800 feet in the Amyndeon region of northern Greece. Low yields of Syrah and Merlot are blended with Xinomavro to create Alpha One Red, a dark, intense wine with spiced, dark cherry fruit with peppery nuances and a firm structure.

Food pairings: Roasted red meats, such as beef or lamb
Vintage years: 2006, 2005, 2004

8 Biblia Chora Estate Red, Macedonia

Modern fruit-forward styles from this recently established operation with 400 acres of vines on the flinty soils of Mount Pangeon in Macedonia. A blend of Merlot and Cabernet Sauvignon, the wine has bright plum and cherry fruit and herbal and minerally notes with velvety tannins.

Food pairings: Tomato-based fish stews
VIntage years: 2004, 2003, 2002

10 Kir-Yianni Dyo Elies, Vin de Pays d'Imathia, Naoussa

Owned by the Boutari family, Kir-Yianni is high in the mountains of Macedonia. This delicious blend of Syrah and Merlot with local variety Xinomavro has blackberry and plum fruit with lively, clean acidity and structured tannins.

Food pairings: Slow-cooked lamb
Vintage years: 2006, 2005, 2004

Agiorgitiko growing near Patras, Peloponnese, Greece

Lebanon

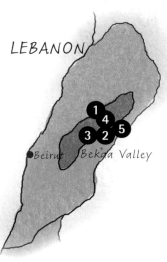

Throughout the years of conflict, one producer in Lebanon, Serge Hochar, captured the world's admiration by continuing to produce wine and crossing checkpoints with truckloads of grapes between vineyard and winery. Now other producers are moving forward and capturing fresh, concentrated flavors. Lebanon's vineyards are concentrated in the Bekaa Valley and in the hills above Zahlé, where a combination of high altitudes and warm sunshine produce dense, opulent, elegant wines from Bordeaux and Rhône varietals.

Lavender grows alongside vines at the beautiful Tanaïl Property in Bekaa Valley—home of Massaya wine

❶ Château Musar, Cuvée Reserve, Bekaa Valley

Made from a blend of Cabernet Sauvignon, Cinsault, and Carignan from vineyards at 3,000 feet altitude in the Bekaa Valley, this is Lebanon's most celebrated wine. Deep, sweet, plummy fruit with notes of tea and herbs and a spicy, alcoholic finish.

Food pairings: Slow-baked lamb
Vintage years: 2003, 2000, 1996

❷ Massaya Classic Red, Bekaa Valley

A revitalized estate in the north of the Bekaa Valley, and now with three partners from top French estates providing expertise. The Classic wine, made from a blend of Cabernet Sauvignon, Cinsault, Grenache, and others, is elegant with rich chocolaty fruit; meaty, spicy notes; and supple tannins.

Food pairings: Broiled spiced chicken
Vintage years: 2006, 2004, 2001

❹ Château Ksara, Bekaa Valley

Established in 1857, Lebanon's largest estate has over 1,000 acres of vines at five sites within the Bekaa Valley. This red, the main château wine, is a blend of Cabernet Sauvignon, Merlot, and Petit Verdot. It has deep, red berry fruit and a rustic, complex finish.

Food pairings: Spiced red beans and lentils
Vintage years: 2004, 2003, 2002

❸ Clos St Thomas, Château St Thomas, Bekaa Valley

With 125 acres of vineyards overlooking the Bekaa Valley, Clos St Thomas produces New World–style wines from a blend of Cabernet Sauvignon, Merlot, and Syrah. This wine has warm red fruit aromas, harmonious cassis and plum flavors, with velvety tannins.

Food pairings: Paprika and cumin-spiced chicken
Vintage years: 2001, 2000, 1999

❺ Château Kefraya Lebanon, Bekaa Valley

Overlooking the Bekaa Valley at around 3,000 feet above sea level, vineyards at this large estate are planted on thin clay and limestone soil. Cabernet Sauvignon with Syrah, Mourvèdre, and Carignan combine to produce a wine with dark, spicy blackberry fruit and firm tannins.

Food pairings: Stuffed grape leaves
Vintage years: 2002, 2001, 2000

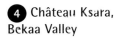

Israel

Despite a history of vines and winemaking that predates
Europe by 2,000 years, and a worldwide demand for
kosher wines, Israel's wine industry is comparatively
small. The largest wine regions are in the south, in
Shomrom and Samson, where robust reds are produced in
a warm Mediterranean climate. Farther inland, on the
Judean Hills just north of Jerusalem, the cooler climate and
thin stony soil produce higher-quality wines with more
complexity. The main quality wine region lies in the north, in
Galilee, where altitude tempers the daytime heat and cool
nights allow slower ripening.

Volcanic soil in the Galilee produces quality Cabernets, Merlots, and Syrahs

1 Carmel Private Collection Cabernet Sauvignon, Galilee

Founded in 1882 by Baron Edmond de Rothschild, Carmel is one of the largest producers and exporters of wine in Israel. Quality has improved greatly in recent years. This Cabernet Sauvignon has dark red fruit flavors and chocolate, with light spice on the finish.

Food pairings: Herb-roasted chicken
Vintage years: 2006, 2005, 2004

2 Recanati Cabernet Sauvignon Reserve, Galilee

This winery was founded in 2000 with vineyards in Upper Galilee. Made from grapes grown at 2,500 feet on two soil types—chalk and iron-rich terra rossa—this wine is firm and juicy with plum and cherry fruit, chocolate and mint notes, and a harmonious finish.

Food pairings: Cumin-spiced lamb
Vintage years: 2005, 2004, 2002

4 Golan Heights Winery, Yarden Cabernet Sauvignon El Rom, Galilee

Yarden is the flagship label at this modern winery high in the Golan Heights. Here high-altitude vineyards and cool summers produce quality wine. This shows crisp raspberry, blueberry, and red plum fruit with touches of mint and dark chocolate.

Food pairings: Filet mignon
Vintage years: 2004, 2003

3 Dalton Reserve Cabernet Sauvignon, Galilee

Established in 1993, this is one of the few estate wineries in Israel to be surrounded by its own vineyards. Deep red fruit and vanilla on the nose leads to rounded smooth fruit with smooth defined tannins.

Food pairings: Vegetable-bean soup
Vintage years: 2006, 2005, 2002

5 Domaine du Castel Grand Vin, Judean Hills

A small, high-quality, family-run estate in the Judean Hills making elegant stylish reds. The blend of Cabernet Sauvignon, Merlot, and Petit Verdot, aged two years in new French oak, has dried plum and cherry fruit, concentrated mineral and herbal notes, with smooth, supple tannins.

Food pairings: Broiled filet mignon
Vintage years: 2005, 2004, 2003

Germany

World-famous for the quality of its white wines, Germany also makes an increasing amount of red wine. The main grape variety is Pinot Noir, known in Germany as Spätburgunder, which produces gentle, fragrant wines. Other varieties include the deep-colored, soft-textured Dornfelder, a result of crossing the Portugieser grape with other German grapes and Lemberger. Red wines are found mainly in the southern region of Baden, but are also scattered across the whole vineyard area including the Ahr, Rheingau, and Franken. These wines are fashionable in their own country—exports are low and prices are high.

Harvest in Baden

1 Rudolf Fürst, Centgrafenberg Spätburgunder, Franken

Half of this 37-acre estate is planted with red varieties, principally Pinot Noir, which acquires more depth and complexity here than many other German Pinots. Aged in large casks and barriques, this has cherry and damson fruit, with weight, intensity, and fine tannins.

Food pairings: Peppered beef or venison
Vintage years: 2006, 2005, 2004

2 Meyer-Nakel, Spätburgunder, Ahr

The Ahr is the source of some of Germany's finest Spätburgunders, and Werner Nakel consistently makes top-ranking wines. This, the basic red, is fragrant with cherry and red currant fruit with a silky texture. Blauschiefer and Dernauer Pfarrwingert provide increasing complexity at a price.

Food pairings: Roast pork loin
Vintage years: 2006, 2005, 2004

4 Bernhard Huber, Spätburgunder Junge Reben, Baden

This property, based on the limestone and loess soil of southern Baden, moved to bottling its own wines in the 1980s and has developed a reputation for its Pinots. Bold in style, even from young vines, the wines are ripe, balanced, and toasty.

Food pairings: Roast chicken
Vintage years: 2006, 2005, 2004

3 Friedrich Becker, Spätburgunder, Pfalz

This 36-acre estate in the southern part of the Pfalz straddles the French border with some vineyards lying in Alsace. There is a definite focus on red wines here, with Spätburgunder ripening well to give rounded, cherry-scented fruit and soft, supple tannins.

Food pairings: Broiled salmon with roasted root vegetables
Vintage years: 2007, 2006, 2005

5 August Kesseler, Cuvée Max, Rheingau

Unusual for the Rheingau, the dominant variety at this 35-acre estate is Pinot Noir. Cuvée Max is made in a Burgundian style, with open, large vat fermentation and hand punch-downs. Barrique maturation yields a wine with herb-sprinkled cherry fruit with a sweet, juicy palate.

Food pairings: Herb-baked white fish or seared wild duck
Vintage years: 2005, 2004, 2003

Austria

With a new generation of winemakers in Austria, quality is to the fore, with excellent white wines, both dry and sweet, but the real progress has been with reds. Local grape varieties, such as the robust Blaufränkisch, the soft cherry-fruited Zweigelt, and the brambly, structured St. Laurent, provide most of the red wines. The main region for red wine is in eastern Austria, south of Vienna in Burgenland. Around Neusiedlersee, the warm shallow lake moderates temperatures in fall, providing long, gentle ripening, which makes it suitable for red grapes. Farther south in Mittelburgenland is another enclave for Blaufränkisch.

AUSTRIA

Neusiedlersee

7 4
3 1
8 5 2
9 6 10

Burgenland

Zweigelt grapes provide a soft cherry fruit flavor

❶ Sepp, Moser Zweigelt Neusiedlersee

Soft, rounded, dark cherry and bramble fruit with a touch of white pepper and spice on the finish in this good value wine. Sepp Moser is a large independent producer with estates in Kremstal for white wines and in Burgenland for reds.

Food pairings: Beef or eggplant pasta parmagiana
Vintage years: 2007, 2006, 2005

❷ Pöckl, Zweigelt, Neusiedlersee

Rene Pöckl is now the winemaker at this red-wine estate. Zweigelt is good value wine with bright berry and raspberry fruit, spice, and a touch of smoke. Trade up to the Admiral, the Zweigelt–Cabernet Merlot blend, to taste one of Austria's best reds.

Food pairings: Herb-stuffed pork loin
Vintage years: 2007, 2006, 2005

❹ Juris, St Laurent Selection, Neusiedlersee

Axel Stiegelmar is the current winemaker at this long-established family estate, which has gained a reputation for its red wines. This St Laurent wine is a lush, fruit-driven wine, full of dark plum and cassis flavors with a touch of spice and mint.

Food pairings: Firm white fish, provençal-style
Vintage years: 2006, 2005, 2004

❸ Kracher, Zweigelt TBA No. 1 Nouvelle Vague, Neusiedlersee

Kracher is a sweet wine specialist making tiny quantities of a sweet Zweigelt. Grapes remain on the vines until raisined and then fermented to around 10 percent alcohol, leaving incredible sweetness, balanced by keen acidity. Unusual and very expensive.

Food pairings: Cherry and chocolate dessert
Vintage years: 2005, 2004, 2002

❺ Feiler-Artinger, Solitaire, Neusiedlersee-Hügelland

Reds have become increasingly important at this estate. This barrique-aged Blaufränkisch, Cabernet Sauvignon, and Merlot blend has achieved almost cult status with deep cherry, plum, and chocolate notes.

Food pairings: Chicken or pheasant casserole
Vintage years: 2007, 2006, 2005

6 Schiefer, Blaufränkisch Eisenberg, Süd-burgenland

Just 13 acres of vines produce quality reds from Blaufränkisch grapes grown on schistous soils in the southern part of Burgenland. The wines have rich, deep cherry and bramble fruit with a ripe, tannic backbone.

Food pairings: Chicken casserole
Vintage years: 2006, 2005, 2004

7 Anita and Hans Nittnaus, Neusiedlersee Pannobile

This estate is planted principally with Blaufränkisch and Zweigelt red grapes, which ripen east of Neusiedlersee. Pannobile is predominately Zweigelt and has blueberry and blackberry fruit, with light spice notes and a coffee, chocolate finish.

Food pairings: Roast duck
Vintage years: 2005, 2004, 2003

9 Krutzler, Blaufränkisch Südburgenland

With vineyards on iron-rich soils in a southeast-facing amphitheater, protected from winds, Blaufränkisch grapes ripen to perfection, providing intense plum and cherry fruit. Move up to the fantastic Cabernet-enhanced Perwolf if the budget allows.

Food pairings: Broiled calves' liver with onions
VIntage years: 2006, 2005, 2004

8 Ernst Triebaumer, Gmark Blaufränkisch, Neusiedlersee-Hügelland

One of the best-known names in Burgenland, with vineyards spread out across the western side of the Neusiedlersee, facing the morning sun. This Blaufränkisch has fresh raspberry and cherry fruit with a touch of licorice and a snappy finish.

Food pairings: Mild Indian-spiced vegetable casserole
Vintage years: 2006, 2005, 2003

10 Arachon, T–FX–T Evolution, Burgenland

Named after the three leading winemakers who are the founders of this project, this dense, plummy, spice-edged wine is made from Blaufränkisch and other grapes grown to exacting standards. Meticulous winemaking and 20 months of barrique aging make this a wine for aging.

Food pairings: Roast beef
Vintage years: 2005, 2004, 2001

6 ||| 7 ||| 8 || 9 || 10 ||||

A vineyard in winter, Raiding, Burgenland

index

280

picture credits

The images in this book are used with the permission of the copyright holders stated below. (Images are listed by page number.) All other illustrations and pictures are © Quintet Publishing Limited. While every effort has been made to credit contributors, Quintet would like to apologize should there have been any omissions or errors and would be pleased to make the appropriate correction for future editions of the book.

6 Holler, Hendrik / FoodCollection / Stockfood America; 8 Lehmann, Jörg / Stockfood America Shutterstock; 12 New, Myles / FoodCollection / Stockfood America; 17 Faber, Armin / Stockfood America; 19 Siffert, Hans-Peter / Stockfood America; 21 New, Myles / FoodCollection / Stockfood America; 23 Lehmann, Jörg / Stockfood America; 25 Matassa, Mario / Stockfood America; 26 Faber, Armin / Stockfood America (left) Kern, Thorsten / Stockfood America (center); 27 Faber, Armin / Stockfood America; 29 Lehmann, Jörg / Stockfood America; 30 Carriere, James / Stockfood America; 33 Faber, Armin / Stockfood America; 37 Morris, Steven / Stockfood America; 42 FoodPhotogr. Eising / Stockfood America; 45 Lehmann, Jörg / Stockfood America; 46 Westermann, Jan-Peter / Stockfood America; 56 Holler, Hendrik / Stockfood America; 58 Siffert, Hans-Peter / Stockfood America; 61 Faber, Armin / Stockfood America; 62 Matsuyama, Keiko / Stockfood America; 67 Holler, Hendrik / Stockfood America; 68 Holler, Hendrik / Stockfood America; 71 Holler, Hendrik / Stockfood America; 72 Holler, Hendrik / Stockfood America; 75 Faber, Armin / Stockfood America; 79 Morris, Steven / Stockfood America; 80 Holler, Hendrik / Stockfood America; 82 Columbia Crest Winery 84 Shutterstock; 86 Shutterstock; 88 Shutterstock; 90 Shutterstock; 94 Siffert, Hans-Peter / Stockfood America; 97 Holler, Hendrik / Stockfood America; 98 Morris, Steven / Stockfood America; 100 Faber, Armin / Stockfood America; 104 Lehmann, Herbert / Stockfood America; 107 Siffert, Hans-Peter / Stockfood America; 108 Lehmann, Herbert / Stockfood America; 111 Faber, Armin / Stockfood America; 112 Faber, Armin / Stockfood America; 114 Faber, Armin / Stockfood America; 120 Morris, Steven / Stockfood America; 123 Morris, Steven / Stockfood America; 124 Morris, Steven / Stockfood America; 126 Morris, Steven / Stockfood America; 128 Siffert, Hans-Peter / Stockfood America; 130 Holler, Hendrik / Stockfood America; 132 Holler, Hendrik / Stockfood America; 135 Holler, Hendrik / Stockfood America; 136 Siffert, Hans-Peter / Stockfood America; 138 Holler, Hendrik / Stockfood America; 141 Holler, Hendrik / Stockfood America; 144 Siffert, Hans-Peter / Stockfood America; 146 Holler, Hendrik / Stockfood America; 148 Siffert, Hans-Peter / Stockfood America; 150 Morris, Steven / Stockfood America; 154 Faber, Armin / Stockfood America; 157 Holler, Hendrik / Stockfood America; 158 Siffert, Hans-Peter / Stockfood America; 160 Faber, Armin / Stockfood America; 162 Holler, Hendrik / Stockfood; 168 Siffert, Hans-Peter / Stockfood America; 173 Siffert, Hans-Peter / Stockfood America; 174 Morris, Steven / Stockfood America; 176 Morris, Steven / Stockfood America; 178 Lehmann, Jörg / Stockfood America; 180 Siffert, Hans-Peter / Stockfood America; 183 Lehmann, Jörg / Stockfood America; 186 Lehmann, Jörg / Stockfood America; 189 Siffert, Hans-Peter / Stockfood America; 190 Siffert, Hans-Peter / Stockfood America; 193 Lehmann, Jörg / Stockfood America; 194 Grilly, Bernard / Stockfood America; 196 Siffert, Hans-Peter / Stockfood America; 198 Lehmann, Jörg / Stockfood America 202 Holler, Hendrik / Stockfood America; 204 Faber, Armin / Stockfood America; 207 Holler, Hendrik / Stockfood America; 208 Holler, Hendrik / Stockfood America; 211 Lehmann, Jörg / Stockfood America; 212 Lehmann, Jörg / Stockfood America; 214 Lehmann, Jörg / Stockfood; 216 Siffert, Hans-Peter / Stockfood America; 218 Lehmann, Jörg / Stockfood 222 Faber, Armin / Stockfood America; 225 Siffert, Hans-Peter / Stockfood America; 226 Faber, Armin / Stockfood America; 228 Siffert, Hans-Peter / Stockfood America, 231 Siffert, Hans-Peter / Stockfood America; 232 Siffert, Hans-Peter / Stockfood America; 235 Siffert, Hans-Peter / Stockfood America; 236 Siffert, Hans-Peter / Stockfood America; 239 Siffert, Hans-Peter / Stockfood America; 242 Holler, Hendrik / Stockfood America; 245 Faber, Armin / Stockfood America; 246 Holler, Hendrik / Stockfood America; 248 Holler, Hendrik / Stockfood America; 250 Morris, Steven / Stockfood America; 252 Faber, Armin / Stockfood America; 254 Faber, Armin / Stockfood America; 256 Faber, Armin / Stockfood America; 258 Siffert, Hans-Peter / Stockfood America; 261 Faber, Armin / Stockfood America; 264 Lehmann, Jörg / Stockfood America; 265 Lehmann, Jörg / Stockfood America; 268 Massaya & Co.; 270 Shutterstock; 272 Holler, Hendrik / Stockfood America; 274 Faber, Armin / Stockfood America; 276 Faber, Armin / Stockfood America.

acknowledgments

The author would like to thank contributors Natasha Hughes and Wink Lorch.

Quintet would like to thank the following wine agencies and vineyards who helped with the wine bottle image research in the book: ABS Wines; Accent Communications; Adnams; Bibendum Wine; Boutinot Limited; Calera Wines; Chateau Les Ormes de Pez; Chateau Musar; Cono Sur Winery; Dedicated Wines; Domaines Ott*; Enotria Wines; Fells; Felton Road; Fields Morris Verdin Wines; François Lurton; Great Western Wine; H&H Bancroft Wines; Halewood International; Hilltop Wines; Inniskillin Wines; Layment & Shaw Wine Merchants; La Sauvageonne; Les Caves de Pyrene; Liberty Wines; Limm Communications; Maison Sichel; Moet Hennessey; Morgan Winery; Moreno Wines; Negociants; Patriarche Wines; PLB Group; Pol Roger; Pontet-Canet; R&R Teamwork; Raisin Social; Richards Walford & Company; Seckford Agencies; Spear Communication; Thorman Hunt & Co; Vinoceros; Wine Partners; Yamas Wines; Yvon Mau.